THE THOUGHT LEADER WAY

I0479702

INDIA • SINGAPORE • MALAYSIA

Notion Press

No.8, 3rd Cross Street
CIT Colony, Mylapore
Chennai, Tamil Nadu – 600004

First Published by Notion Press 2020
Copyright © Dr. Karthik Nagendra 2020
All Rights Reserved.

ISBN 978-1-64951-778-4

THE THOUGHT LEADER WAY

Leading Your Business with Thought Leadership in an Altered World

DR. KARTHIK NAGENDRA

INDIA • SINGAPORE • MALAYSIA

INDICACADEMY

INDIC PLEDGE

————◆◆————

- *I celebrate our civilisational identity, continuity & legacy in thought, word and deed.*

- *I believe our indigenous thought has solutions for the global challenges of health, happiness, peace and sustainability.*

- *I shall seek to preserve, protect and promote this heritage and in doing so,*
  - *discover, nurture and harness my potential,*
  - *connect, cooperate and collaborate with fellow seekers,*
  - *advance diversity and inclusivity in the society.*

ABOUT INDIC ACADEMY

————◆◆————

Indic Academy is a non-traditional 'university' for traditional knowledge. We seek to bring about a global renaissance based on Indic civilizational and indigenous thought. We are pursuing a multidimensional strategy across time, space and cause by establishing centers of excellence, transforming intellectuals and building an ecosystem.

Indic Academy is pleased to support this book.

Dedicated to the thought leader in my life: My Dad

Contents

Foreword

Business relationships are based on trust. That you will be able to deliver what you promise. In many B2B transactions there is no way to prove that the product or service will work before you actually buy, because it will have to be installed in your organization and run with your inputs.

Sometimes the results vary on the usage conditions. There are many considerations for buyers to be wary of promises.

As I discovered in my roles heading global branding for Infosys, and later as Chief Marketing Officer for Wipro Technologies, the only way to build trust in this situation is to position your business and key resources as experts. Experts who can deal with whatever is thrown at them and design a winning solution. The area of marketing that deals with this projection of expertise is Thought Leadership. It is often confused with content marketing but it is a superset of that and involves more than just content and dissemination. For example, awards, patents, events are also part of a thought leadership portfolio.

Given the importance of the topic, this standalone book is a valuable companion to anyone interested in Thought Leadership. Karthik Nagendra leverages his long experience and expertise in Thought Leadership, both as my colleague at Wipro and later as a consultant and advisor to multiple organisations, to deliver a book that covers the breadth of the topic at depth.

The case studies span a range of organizations and include both Business to Business (B2B) and Business to Consumer (B2C) examples. As Karthik explains in the book, a well run thought leadership program can accelerate adoption, create a brand preference and generate a price premium for your product or service.

Karthik's writing style communicates key concepts simply and the numerous diagrams, charts and templates help make the content more actionable and easy to consume.

The book is ideal for anyone seeking to understand how they can communicate expertise in a marketing context, or looking for new ideas to rejuvenate their content and thought leadership programs. It is also the perfect read for anyone seeking to learn about this important area of marketing. There are great learnings for consultants to position themselves as experts too.

The success of a marketing campaign rests on the quality of the content, and quality content is created by a well run Thought Leadership program. I wish you all the best in your thought leadership journey.

Jessie Paul

CEO- Paul Writers

Author of bestseller - No Money Marketing

PART I

EVOLUTION OF THE NEW CONSUMER: TRANSFORMING CUSTOMERS FROM 1.0 TO 2.0

Introduction

"Thought Leaders – informed leaders in a niche,
the go-to people in their field of expertise"

Do you take TV spots, news ads, and billboards at face value?

Neither do most people today. Spurts in technological advancements have transformed the marketing landscape. At the fore, traction through clichéd and hackneyed guarantees is dwindling because, subconsciously, we question the premise of most advertisers' claims. We look for brand advocates that address the basic ingredient of any seller-buyer relationship – **trust**. Finding dependable brand advocates is driven by sound research, domain expertise, innovative thinking, and key stakeholder engagement that aim to establish the brand as an expert advisor and partner. These experts are referred to as *thought leaders*. They are "trusted sources" that customers turn to when they are ready to step up and transact (after being educated and nurtured in their area of need/interest by these thought leaders). Simply put, thought leadership can be considered as a form of educative marketing in which experts engage with prospective customers in a non-promotional way and in industry-oriented conversations.

So, where does thought leadership fall in the modern ethos of B2B marketing?

Today, it pays to be an influential expert in a niche domain – a surefire way to get rewarded with more business than your competitors. This is an essential tenet that B2B firms must consider, especially companies that sell largely intangible services where a client hires your firm for intellectual capital – the unique amalgamation of people, processes, expertise, and ideas that shape your firm. Building a reputation and awareness with no strings attached is vital to attracting customers looking for brand connoisseurs.

**BY SHIFTING FOCUS FROM GLAMORIZING
A PRODUCT TO ESTABLISHING CREDIBILITY,
THOUGHT LEADERSHIP MARKETING REAFFIRMS THE
"HUMANITY" IN THE BRAND-CUSTOMER RELATIONSHIP.**

The term 'thought leadership' was first coined in 1994 by Joel Kurtzman, editor-in-chief of Strategy+Business. According to Kurtzman, a thought leader is recognized by peers, customers, and industry experts as an influencer who deeply understands the business they are in, the needs of their customers, and the broader landscape in which they operate. They have distinctively original ideas, unique points of view, and insights. This concept emerged at the dawn of the internet's explosion. The internet revolution accelerated and expanded opportunities for circulating ideas, dramatically growing the potential and impact of thought leadership. Over time, thought leadership evolved from a personal platform to a credible business practice with real, tangible value. Thought leadership content is often a double-edged sword. When done successfully, it can make specialized expertise accessible to strengthen a business's reputation and impel better engagement that leads to real business results. However, when done poorly, it could mar a brand's reputation and cripple a company's sales efforts.

Thought Leadership Content – Boon or Bane?

Yes, thought leadership content can stimulate buyers, shift their perception of what thought leadership entails, and fortify its impact throughout the customer journey. It helps brands win, retain, and grow their business. Salespersons have often underestimated the potential impact thought leadership could have on demand generation and sales efforts compared to real feedback from B2B buyers. Furthermore, consumption is on the rise. Decision makers are willing to gain valuable insights if the vision and quality aren't compromised. These decision makers use thought leadership as an important way to vet companies they're keen to work with. They are willing to pay higher premiums to collaborate with organizations that articulate a clear value proposition through thought leadership as it drives growth with existing customers as well.

Quality thought leadership content pieces are a rare commodity. Most B2B marketers lose out on capitalizing the full-funnel potential of thought leadership; the influence it could have on sales is a lot greater than most marketers realize. In a nutshell, this could refer to freebies that organizations or individuals produce on a topic in their area of expertise under the premise that other people could benefit from their perspective. Thought leadership is long-term – the aim is to garner trust by establishing a client brand as an advisor and expert. It is about sculpting the 'soul' of your business around which all branding and marketing decisions should be aligned. You should strive to create long-term credibility for brands as trusted advisors. How? Increase visibility and stand with the people who matter by influencing them as an advisor, strategist, and advocator.

My Journey with Thought Leadership

With close to two decades of core marketing experience that primarily focuses on positioning content strategy, executive communication, and thought leadership marketing, I've enjoyed working on multiple award-winning marketing programs with leading brands like MeriTrac, India's largest skill assessment company, where I had the opportunity to work on India's first talent pool report; Wipro Technologies, where I was instrumental in setting up the Wipro Council for Industry Research to drive thought leadership by collaborating with leading global Ivy League universities; and at Accenture, where we ran its first India-centric campaign driven by research and thought leadership. Through this journey, I discovered the potential for thought leadership marketing and identified the gaps to deliver it. This led me to start Thought Starters with the singular mission of helping businesses transform from sellers to influencers by guiding them in unearthing their "big idea" through an approach that is grounded in facts. Working with leading universities and research firms on a global scale helped us in providing the best practices and insights to customers across sectors. Over the years, I have been recognized for my contribution to the field of thought leadership marketing through various awards - Top 10 content marketing professionals in Japan and APAC by CMS Asia and among Top 10 Marketing Consultants in India by CEO Magazine, among others.

AT THOUGHTSTARTERS, OUR DOMAIN EXPERTISE EMPOWERS OUR CLIENTS, RANGING FROM SMALL AND MEDIUM ENTERPRISES TO FORTUNE 500 COMPANIES AROUND THE GLOBE, TO PLAN AND EXECUTE EFFECTIVE, LONG-TERM MARKETING STRATEGIES.

What Can You Expect From This Book?

This book can be best described as an attempt to help you delve into what thought leadership is, the bigger picture of how thought leadership marketing is not just a moving cog in the marketing wheel, but a very important aspect of acquiring new business in the B2B landscape – by instilling trust. I've tried to commit this thinking to paper, partly to help you follow my lead in discovering what thought leadership means to me, and how it can be leveraged successfully to build a thriving buyer base by onboarding leaders and experts in various industries. This book can be adopted as a manual by any aspirational B2B marketer looking to test the waters in thought leadership marketing and, further, serve as a guide to give your business the veneer of excellence. I strongly believe that thought leadership enhances a brand's reputation and yields tangible business impact by capitalizing on collaboration.

- From a marketing professional, practitioner and observer, this book will be useful for all students and practitioners of marketing
- Filled with concepts, frameworks explained through real examples and cases, the book focuses on insights, informative interviews with experts
- Covers a vast spectrum of subjects like content strategy, research, influencer engagement, content marketing along with measurement metrics for success

Customer 2.0: Changing Buying Behavior

In the past, traditional sales tactics such as cold calling, TV advertising, and stellar elevator pitches were an effective means of marketing, and in some cases even considered best practice. During this period, buyers needed a salesperson to educate them on products and services. The 1990s saw companies commit substantial budgets to their marketing efforts. The marketing landscape was brimming with opportunities and it sustained unrivalled success as a result of massive press coverage for events such as product launches, trade shows etc. Marketers didn't have it easy, but things seemed straightforward. If you wanted to connect with a prospect, the tried-and-tested method was to push your message in their face via print media and display advertising. Along with scant data and sparse innovation, excessive brand messaging was the standard in majority of B2B marketing companies.

TODAY, THE MODUS OPERANDI OF B2B MARKETING HAS INTENSIFIED AND, OF COURSE, THOUGHT LEADERSHIP AS A CRITICAL COMPONENT IN THE BUYER FRAMEWORK HAS BECOME VERY VITAL TO MARKETING SUCCESS.

Let's rewind the clock to 2008. B2B buyers, comprising mostly the boomer generation, worked collectively towards making the purchasing decisions for their companies. These buyers were ushered through their customer journey by salespersons who were tasked with only closing deals. B2B marketing teams were responsible for generating quality leads and the sales teams were tasked with converting these leads into potential customers. Information was sparse to the average buyer, and they relied on sales teams to educate them on various solutions. The marketing playbook has since changed. Salespersons have been unseated as information gatekeepers. Over time, consuming information and knowledge about products and services has evolved beyond seeking the expertise of one individual or team.

The Digital Era

Fast forward to 2020, and the status quo has changed – *marketing is all-digital*. The perception of being dependent on sales personnel for making informed decisions stands debunked. B2B buying has evolved significantly in the last decade. Today, B2B buyers belong to the millennial cohort and are inherently tech-savvy. The arrival of smartphones has led people to instant, accessible internet everywhere. The power now rests in the palm of the buyer – a manifestation of Forrester's 2011 declaration of the "Age of the Customer". This shift in power, brought upon by technological innovation, instant access to information, and a systemic overhaul of the existing customer experience model has molded today's B2B buyers into independent, informed, experience-driven customers.

MODERN B2B BUYER JOURNEYS ENTAIL MYRIAD OPTIONS WHERE A BUYER CAN SIFT BETWEEN VENDOR WEBSITES, SEARCH ENGINES, SOCIAL MEDIA, AND ONLINE FORUMS TO GATHER ALL THE INFORMATION THEY DESIRE WITHOUT ENGAGING A SALESPERSON.

The biggest takeaway from the change in B2B marketing dynamics is that the control is now in the hands of the buyer. With the internet at their fingertips, in-depth research and due diligence that can be undertaken on a granular level, the requirement of a mere sales pitch for any product/service gets tossed out the window.

Buyer purchasing behavior has changed significantly. B2B buyers have become more empowered. Furthermore, their values and perspectives are evolving as the younger generation becomes a larger, and more influential portion of the workforce. We now see five generations of professionals in the workforce for the first time in history. With baby boomers and Gen X'ers on the verge of retirement, they are making way for millennials – these are people with different needs, priorities, and buying methods.

What we see today is a labyrinth of options in which a tectonic shift in power has shaped these buyers into independent advocates through the eruption of technological innovation and an overhaul of the contemporary customer experience. The future will intrigue, challenge, and inspire people – thought leaders can start relationships and engage in blue-ocean strategy that focuses on themselves and their clients as opposed to simply churning out ideas and curated content that showcases others' ideas. This requires a sense of tunnel vision to achieve mastery in a discipline by answering the biggest questions on the minds of your buyers, relinquishing control, and letting your clients set the agenda. Be an idea engine and aggregate followers around ideas to influence and inspire. The B2B buyers of today are evolving – they like to hustle; they need someone who cuts to the chase or they are lost forever as potential customers.

Fig 8. Buying environment insight

6. Forrester: Death of a B2B salesman:
Two Years Later: Andy Hoar: March 29, 2017.

Industrial Consumerism Experience the New Normal **14**

Forrester's 2011 declaration of the "Age of the Customer

Need to Reinvent the B2B Consumer Experience

KEEPING UP WITH AN EVOLVING BUYER PSYCHOLOGY

Why is the buyer psychology evolving?

Emotion and Information. B2B decision making – not just the information, but the emotional connect the information delivers.

B2B buying habits are no longer just about fact-based, rational decisions based on weighing pros and cons, data, and comparative analysis. B2B buyers are now more connected, impatient, impulsive, and better informed than their predecessors. Companies that don't address the emotional aspect of buying are in for an uphill battle to keep up with changing buyer behavior. Buying decisions are often the outcome of a change in a customer's emotions. Information influences the rationale and helps change an emotional state but, it is the emotion that matters the most, and not the information.

American author and long-term columnist, (Geoffrey James, 2012) stated in an Inc. blog that buying decisions unfold from interplay of six emotions:

1. **Greed.** "If I make a decision now, I will be rewarded."
2. **Fear.** "If I don't make a decision now, I'm toast."
3. **Altruism.** "If I make a decision now, I will help others."
4. **Envy.** "If I don't make a decision now, my competition will win."
5. **Pride.** "If I make a decision now, I will look smart."
6. **Shame.** "If I don't make a decision now, I will look stupid."

Every successful sales approach either creates or augments one of these six emotional states. When a combination of these emotions is present in the mind of the buyer, a buying decision becomes inevitable. The challenge is to leverage the customer's belief system to drive decision-making – through extensive research.

B2B buying decisions are personal. This stems from a natural cognitive bias that influences what we determine to be a favorable option based on personal need and consequence. Most B2B marketing efforts are targeted to influence potential customers using some form of cognitive bias. These biases exist in the human psyche and can influence a consumer's rationale. These are often done by leveraging tactics such as loss aversion where you create a fallacy of potential loss that would drive a customer to make a purchase, and in-group favoritism where customers buy products which are recommended by friends or social circles. Product or service differentiators should be pushed to create a "wow!" factor – a clear and distinct proposition, delivered in a succinct style; this will be more memorable than bombarding buyers with information. Psychologists have identified two broad categories of decision-making orientations:

- **Aspirational** – individuals who make decisions to enable achievement and positive recognition by others playing to win
- **Preventative** – individuals who make decisions to play to not lose

The more granularly you research your audience, the higher the likelihood of understanding their current state, and the higher the chances of a great customer experience.

Shifting Focus from Lead Generation to Customer Experience

B2B marketers must focus on improving the customer experience due to the ever-changing psyche of today's digitally competent generation. Making it easier for buyers to access information is pivotal to providing a great experience in the initial stage – by unlocking content that would have otherwise been gated. These buyers should be encouraged to access information from websites, white papers, and case studies without being forced to interact with a salesperson. "The challenge is getting consistency around the customer experience – trying to get the different functions working all together instead of in different silos," noted Nicolas Lihou (Head, Global Sales Enablement, Xerox). He further stated that they are less interested in having the best of the best in individuals or functions, but rather get more co-ordination through the different components that affect the customer experience. In other words, work on how you can help customers get the same experience regardless of where the interaction occurs and provide enriching value as they go through their buyer journey.

The traditional approach focused on generating quality leads through lead generation. It was a fallacy to take survey respondents from any campaigns and call them "leads". This strategy meant that companies would push prospective buyers to fill a lead capture form with their contact information and industry in exchange for content, videos, and product demos. Downloading a white paper, watching a demo or signing up for a webinar doesn't always make that person a lead. Usually, potential buyers are in the pre-buying cycle just scouring for information and insights. Without lead scoring to find true, meaningful leads and lead nurturing to develop relationships, it becomes an unproductive cycle of self-serving practices that ultimately yields no tangible outcomes.

Ask yourself. When was the last time you filled out a form to access content from a company you had no interest in purchasing from? Every aspirational marketer wants to build their lead database and prove the value of their marketing automation efforts. And in a bid to achieve that, they often fall short by gating content and other information.

GATING CONTENT IS A STAPLE OF LEAD GENERATION, BUT IT OFTEN WANES POTENTIAL LEADS AS BUYERS AREN'T VERY COMFORTABLE WITH THE EXCHANGE OF PERSONAL DETAILS FOR INFORMATION.

Gating content with a "you scratch my back and I'll scratch yours" outlook helps in acquiring customer details when they opt-in, but beyond that, gated content results in a 80-90% drop in the number of people who want to access that piece of content. Is the compromise worth it? Most experts suggest using a combination of gated and ungated content to connect with decision makers. For instance, you could offer valuable, ungated content to connect with customers on an emotional level that establishes trust and then, engage with them periodically. Once, a relationship has been established, and you have identified your brand loyalists, you could gate thought leadership research reports to create engagement. It is all about finding balance and applying the right strategy at the right time.

The majority of today's B2B buyers are tech-savvy and resourceful enough to stray away from gated content, and often jump ship before going through the rest of the buyer journey. In a world awash with digital content and information, most buyers know they can avoid gated content and seek the information they need elsewhere.

According to a demand generation survey, 87% of the B2B buyers said that the solution provider they chose provided ample content to help them through each stage of the decision-making process. Additionally, according to Think with Google, if buyers are considering you during the research phase, 75% of them are going to visit your site only once.

Ultimately, free access to information allows potential customers to acquire all the content they need resulting in a higher likelihood of them purchasing from the source providing the information. Providing timely, accurate information paired with a great customer experience is crucial to attracting today's B2B buyers.

Now, consider this: your engagement has been timely, your content has hit home, you did an exceptional job of understanding the prospect's pain points and have articulated your value proposition. What's next? Where does the value now lie? For customers, the value comes when your product/service delivers real results for their company. Getting all hands on deck in the post-sales process to set them up for success through sound product/service education, provision of accurate content material, and prompt customer service are all vital to customer satisfaction.

Perfecting the Post-sales Experience – Customer Satisfaction is Key!

B2B consumers expect their enterprise-buying experiences to match the ease and comfort of their consumer-buying experiences. Their experiences as consumers in their personal lives have bled into their professional consumption preferences and, as a result, we see an entire generation of buyers that expect B2B purchases to be as seamless as their B2C purchases.

CONSUMERS YEARN FOR AUTONOMY PRIOR TO MAKING A PURCHASE. REVIEWS, REFERRALS, AND WORD-OF-MOUTH ARE THE STRONGEST INFLUENCERS ON B2B BUYING DECISIONS – HIGH CUSTOMER SATISFACTION IS KEY TO CREATING FUTURE BRAND ADVOCATES.

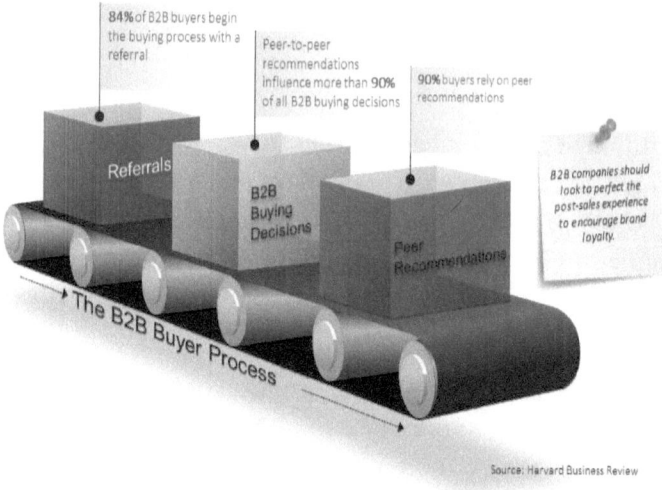

The B2B buying experience will undoubtedly continue to evolve. With a slew of technology tools at our disposal, reaching and influencing target prospects by offering buyers exactly what they are looking for is pivotal to consumer satisfaction. Buyers are now self-sufficient. Empowering your sales teams digitally by letting them gain valuable insights about their targeted cohort of customers is key to keeping up with the changing preferences in today's information-abundant landscape. Staying relevant through digital sales translates to better buyer relationships and sustains brand loyalty.

Digital Selling Driven by Thought Leadership

A few years ago, traditional selling was all about establishing contact with prospective buyers through cold calling. Salespersons had to rely on fickle data. Appointments had to be made to meet with buyers and sales reps often made forced conversations that resulted in unsavory engagement with uninterested customers. This scripted strategy of closing customers is an outdated approach. Old-school sellers have been struggling to impact people the way they did in the past since most people today flock online to make their purchases.

90 % *DECISION MAKERS ADMITTED TO HAVING NEVER RESPONDED TO COLD CALLS*

Today, we exist in a world that's driven by technology. From the way we communicate to the way we go about our shopping – every minute task can be done at the click of a button. Furthermore, the advent of transparent marketplaces coupled with the proliferation of online content, digital communities, and social media is allowing buyers to increasingly self-educate when evaluating a product or service. So, as a result, rather than relying on cold calling, sales teams and leaders are now learning to become trusted guides in their area of expertise and build valuable relationships online. With the massive adoption of digital mediums such as social media, and other digital tools and processes, these trusted leaders or 'thought leaders' have learned to listen and share their opinions with the intended target. They understand the challenges a buyer might face and support these buyers to find a solution. A huge part of digital sales is done via networks such as LinkedIn, Twitter, Facebook, and Instagram.

Infusion of Young Blood

If you work in sales, chances are you might ask, *"why should I learn to engage with my prospect via digital channels?"* The simple answer is that digital selling works. The B2B buyer attitude is very different today compared to the last decade. One crucial driver behind this change is the major increase in the level of competition and disruption in the digital marketplace along with the huge buzz around social media. Customers now have access to a much broader roster of products and services as a result of increasingly shorter product lifecycles and new entrants that entice customers with exciting alternatives to consider.

According to International Data Corporation (IDC), 50-80% of buyers' decision-making processes are complete before a salesperson gets involved

Consequently, B2B buying behavior is starting to look a lot more like B2C. With a teeming generation comprising tech-savvy millennials, the values and perspectives that buyers previously held closely are also evolving. Gen X and baby boomers are slowly giving way to a younger group that has very different needs, priorities, and ways of buying to take over top positions of leadership. For both sales reps and businesses alike, digital selling is rapidly becoming an exciting proposition to drive revenue growth.

SAP is one such company that experienced the shift from established incumbents to young blood firsthand.

"A wave of new competitors trying to eat our lunch forced us to become innovators too," said Phil Lurie – VP of Sales Technology, SAP. "From a sales perspective, we had to equip our people to be able to sell these new solutions and, in many cases, to entirely new customers. At the time, we recognized that traditional ways of selling are no longer effective. Understanding the changing environment, we knew we need to change our sales approach."

SAP realized that to become successful, they had to shift from a traditional approach to becoming digital sellers/leaders in order to grow their revenue streams. Digital selling is a strategy that needs to be adopted in order to survive in a rapidly expanding digital economy. To make it successful, it is important to put a face on your digital selling – a trusty thought leader that customers can relate to.

Adding the Human Touch

The role of a thought leader is to make sure the selling goals are aligned with the overall strategy of the company, garner support with customers in the industry, and provide a sense of direction. Keeping this in mind, you need to ensure that your idea of a thought leader or the thought leader of your choice is not just respected in the organization, but also has a certain level of influence and charisma with your customers as well. He/she needs to understand the goals and outcomes of your digital selling program. A thought leader needs to be leveraged early in the selling process to gain support through practices such as an internal selling program, industry data, and expert quotes. When you promote these facets along with other industry statistics, you establish the thought leader's credibility and persuade customers with hard data and insights.

TO BUILD AN EFFECTIVE DIGITAL SELLING TEAM, SET AN EXAMPLE BY ESTABLISHING A DIGITAL PRESENCE. PERSONALIZING YOUR ENGAGEMENT WITHIN THE NETWORK THROUGH A PERSUASIVE BRAND MESSAGE CEMENTS ONE'S POSITION AS A THOUGHT LEADER. RELATIONSHIPS BUILT THOUGH TRUST HAVE ALWAYS BEEN AT THE CORE OF SELLING.

Having an established social footprint is key to be a successful thought leader in the digital selling landscape. Selecting the right digital channels that work best for you and your organization is strategic – understand what areas of interest you would like to be associated with and how much expertise you have in these areas. Start creating content around these areas and populate the digital platforms that you are most likely to be successful on with this content. These platforms such as LinkedIn, SlideShare or Quora should be used to create high-quality thought leadership content and ideally have a personalized biography that aligns with your company's brand. Customers no longer need navigation to help them traverse through a company's products and solutions. Digital selling proved to be a boon as SAP's Lurie discovered. Lurie reported that by investing in digital selling and empowering his sales teams to become leaders, SAP's sales and marketing pipeline improved by 50 times the amount of money spent.

Digital selling through thought leadership has massive payoffs. It empowers sales and marketing teams by allowing them to gain appropriate insights on relevance to customers – winning their trust, increasing revenue, and ultimately reducing costs.

Marketing + Digital Selling = A Well-oiled Thought Leadership Machine

According to a 2017 Edelman-LinkedIn report,
nine out of ten business decision-makers find thought leadership
important or critical to their decision process, and 82% said that thought
leadership increased their trust in a vendor organization

The consumption of thought leadership content has risen from 50-58% this past year and 55% of decision makers say they use thought leadership as an important way to vet business. Which is still a relatively small number. A lot of brands are still unaware of the impact thought leadership can have on their business. As buyers increasingly help themselves to the wealth of material and knowledge available online, sales should reinvent their role in the demand generation process, and to achieve this, it needs the help of a savvy marketing team. Marketing plays a critical role in developing relevant content to make headway in the sales process. Consider the traditional buyer decision-making process: awareness, information-gathering, evaluation, and selection as shown.

Figure 4: regaining sales' influence in buyer education and evaluation

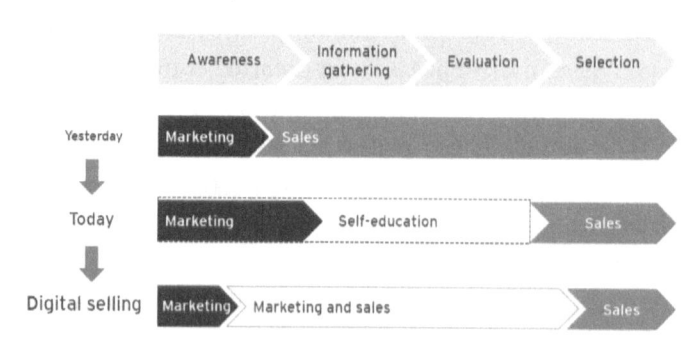

Source: EY

Historically, marketing appeared only in the first phase – generating awareness. Sales owned the rest. Today, marketing is still responsible for awareness and is getting more involved in the information-gathering phase. But, sales, which remains firmly rooted in the selection phase, has effectively lost its place in the two middle phases which customers have taken over for themselves. To regain their influence in information gathering and evaluation, marketing must work closely with sales to help guide customers through these two phases. How?

Need to Realign Marketing, Sales Goals

Figure out where human interaction is most desired and invest there. Companies need to align their marketing and sales goals and metrics to address both verticals working towards the same goal. Doing so will enable them to not only develop high-value marketing content that is relevant to digital sales, but also quantify the content's impact on sales results, and then use an industry leader to heighten its importance to customers. The challenge is to ensure a seamless repetitive cycle from marketing content → customers engagement using thought leadership → increasing digital sales.

Connecting your company's marketing and sales performance with financial outcomes gives you a clearer picture of the company's digital selling efforts. We had seen an example in the previous chapter about a quote by Nicolas Lihou (Head of Global Sales Enablement, Xerox). Revisiting that quote,

---

"The challenge is getting consistency around the customer experience – trying to get the different functions working together instead of in different silos. We are less interested in having the best of the best in individual functions or people and keener on getting much more coordinated through the different components that affect the customer experience. We're working on how we can get the same experience regardless of where customers interact with us and provide richer experiences that add a lot of value through the journey with us."

Delivering a consistent customer experience is synonymous with shifting a customer's perception of your brand and the vision you hold. Consumption of thought leadership content and digital sales through marketing is on the rise. Decision makers are reading about thought leadership much more today than they were before. The probability of B2B buyers spending more to work with companies and thought leaders with a clear vision is a lot higher now. When a thought leader has a clearly articulated vision, buyers are enticed to pay higher digital sales premiums and gain valuable insights.

The rise in video platforms and social networks such as YouTube, LinkedIn, Slideshare, Quora and Twitter have given thought leaders the power to reach out to different customer segments. Being influential in your niche has the potential of generating a significant amount of revenue in the digital space. Trust is an essential component of any economy. We have now learned that digital selling is soon-to-be-the-standard in B2B sales and marketing. Creating an ecosystem to measure how well your content is being consumed by your customers is vital to the success of digital selling. And how best to ensure your content is being consumed? By showcasing thought leadership as a medium to get your unique message across to customers.

1. Brand identity and voice

Every thought leader needs to have an identity – an identity that people relate to. It is the first step towards enhancing your status as a successful thought leader. Your brand voice needs to convey your credibility and authority within your industry. It will determine how your customer engagement unfolds. This would tell you how much trust you have garnered within your customer base. You could start with a simple, yet precise description of your brand – this would set the narrative with customers who are learning about your USPs, i.e. your strengths as a thought leader. Back it up with your skills and experience. You have heard the saying "first impressions last" – it is very important that you have a very clear message through your brand upfront – customers won't look back once you have lost them.

2. Explore topics that set you apart from your competitors

Let's say you have successfully set the narrative for your brand with all the necessary USPs and descriptions. Next, you need to develop and distribute valuable content. Not just blogs that someone might breeze through one evening and not give it a second thought, but relevant topics that need a solution. Some content might require your own opinions (about an industry, a specific product, or a solution) and some require you to be transparent about your own business. Practice what you preach – customers will realize that you're not just a loquacious person with an agenda but an honest practitioner with zeal.

TRANSPARENCY LEADS TO RELATABILITY. RELATABILITY REINFORCES YOUR STANCE AS A THOUGHT LEADER. GETTING CUSTOMERS TO RELATE TO YOUR BRAND MAKES YOU A KNOWLEDGEABLE, TRUSTWORTHY FIGURE IN YOUR INDUSTRY.

---

3. Sublime oratorical skills

As an industry figure, thought leadership requires you to showcase your innovation. Considering that majority of the people today absorb content on mobile devices, blogs wouldn't always do the job. Digital thought leaders need to invest their time and effort in developing podcasts and webinars which are easier for people to digest than a written article (we will explore this topic in detail later).

4. Collaborating with other influencers

If you're just starting out, chances are your outreach is small. Consider reaching out to other established influencers who have a loyal following – these are individuals you could learn from. Following these influencers on LinkedIn, Twitter and other social media platforms where you could ask for advice can help improve the quality of your content and understand your industry better. Networking is vital to getting influencers to know who you are, so that future opportunities for collaboration may appear. Building your relationships with other thought leaders may improve your reputation and, in time, improve your social following.

Forging a partnership with your marketing and sales teams to accurately leverage thought leadership requires both teams to think like customers. There is often a disconnect where marketers do customer research without seeking enough input and salespersons often state that they don't understand the importance of better data. At many B2B companies, both marketing and sales are involved in deciding the right strategy to approach customers. As we stated previously, the key to improving digital sales during your B2B marketing mission is to deliver the right thought leadership content at the right time. A successful digital selling strategy in B2B requires a clear understanding of your ideal customer's needs. Connecting thought leaders to B2B buyers on the right social media platform to build a connection before they buy your product is all about providing resources that let your customers know that they can come to you not only for information on a product but also information about industry trends. If you want to achieve success in your B2B marketing efforts, you need to personalize the experience for your customer. Pushing excess, disconnected content down your customers' throats in a bit to attract them is a thing of the past.

B2B Marketing in the New Normal

With the upsurge in digital channels and technology, B2B buyers now have easy access to information, making it easier for them to derive useful insights about a brand or product. Companies that do not enhance their digital selling efforts in unison with thought leadership stand to risk 10-20% of their revenue. Realistically, the B2B buying journey is tedious. Six out of ten decision makers are often equipped with multiple pieces of information about a complex B2B solution. These changing dynamics make it increasingly difficult for indecisive buyers to make purchases. We know that marketing to businesses is very different from marketing to consumers. B2B marketers will have to put buyers at the core of their purpose. These digitally empowered buyers have changed the roles of sales and marketing. Disruptive models and improvements in technology are changing the digital selling landscape.

Today's marketing multitude largely comprises the millennial cohort – they are tech-savvy, crave personalization, and are not keen on engagement through pre-sales and cold-calling. Modern B2B marketing trends entail creating leverage by enabling and nurturing a community of customers, prospects, partners, and other influencers. The new millennial generation of B2B buying professionals don't conform to the previous generation's preferences and practices, and the traditional brick-and-mortar approach of engaging baby boomers is becoming obsolete. The role of the modern B2B marketing professional is shifting rapidly owing to the explosion of data, analytics, and automation tools. Three trends that are influencing marketing trends now are: personalization, artificial intelligence, and influencer marketing. The chart related to this is given in the next page. So may be we can mention (refer chart in the next page)

Branding involves humanizing your personas. What are the values that are important to this person? When buyer personas and journeys are combined, the result is a clear path to create an engagement strategy for each phase of the buyer journey. *The brand experience must change from customer focused to customer obsessed* (Lori Wizdo, Forrester). Your brand essence is the underlying reason why customers care about your brand – the brand DNA (what makes your company stands for and what differentiates it from your competition). According to marketing experts, adopting new marketing technology and delivering a greater customer experience, standing out online, brand awareness – the proof is in the platform, i.e. thought leadership. Always cherish your customers. Loyal B2B customers drive the economy forwards.

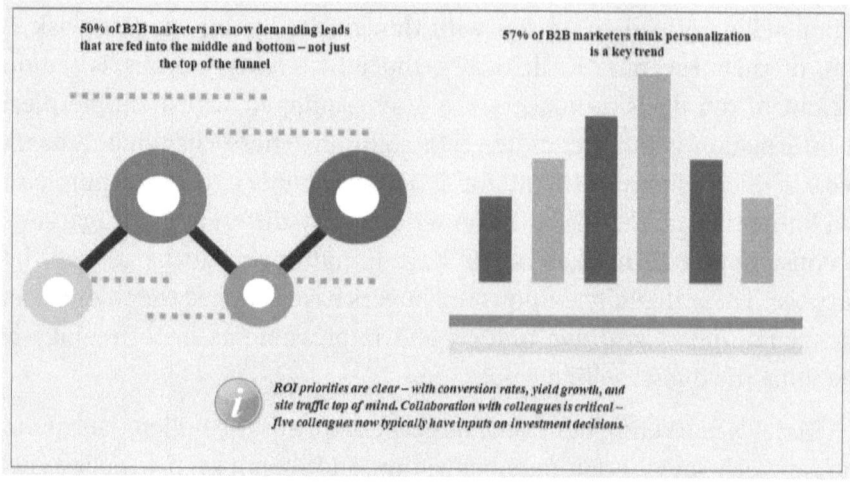

"The difference between business-to-consumer (B2C) and business-to-business (B2B) marketing is that, in the former, the management gets why you're doing it. In B2B it's about convincing the sales guy that people don't just buy based on a list of functionalities"

– Colin Lewis (CMO, OpenJaw Technologies)

B2B marketing is hard. It is very difficult to maintain control of the sales cycle now that buyers have more information available to them. Buyers are changing the way they engage with B2B companies. They are sophisticated. The stakes are much higher now and it requires a great deal of patience.

Challenges Of B2B Marketing

Buyers are performing more searches even before engaging your sales teams, so it is vital to stay one step ahead and offer them answers to their searches. Let's see some real-world challenges faced by executives as stated below.

The Attribution Challenge

"Executives at the round table noted that they find themselves in something of a 'catch 22' situation. On one hand, measurement and attribution is vital to embedding marketing as pivotal to success, but it also suffers from 'Cinderella' syndrome'." Jonathan Palmer, head of global strategy at Omobono explained, "clients don't simply have time to measure a project after we complete it. Pressures of time mean that they look at the numbers, but also, they don't have the time to find out what defines success upfront. How are they going to measure that? It's pushed to the back". Again, the length of the sales cycle seems to be a major roadblock. "It's the driver. In B2C you get a hit every minute. I'd get a text every hour to say what worked and what didn't," said OpenJaw's Lewis, describing his time in consumer marketing. Meanwhile, Lauren Bigland, marketing head at LoopMe, admitted, "tracking is an expense that marketers must pay for, and I find that quite a challenge. The money I spend on tracking I could actually spend on doing an activation."

Changing Channels

The dizzying array of channels available to marketers in general may be responsible for the ongoing attribution debate. Attendees at the roundtable felt that B2B sectors straggled their B2C counterparts in being able to exploit marketing channels to their fullest. "We're not leveraging digital as much as B2C companies are," explained Prachi Prasad, learning and development partner at Vodafone, but she added: "it has shifted in terms of producing more webinars, videos, and podcasts rather than just sponsoring an event." "The customer journey is so different (in B2B and B2C)," added LoopMe's Bigland. "We have a very active social media platform, but I don't think we generate sales from it. As a consumer marketer you can see that sales have been driven (from social) but in B2B, it's interesting but not a key sales driver. The customer journey defines where we have to grow skills."

RESEARCH INDICATES THAT B2B MARKETERS ARE STARTING TO EXPLORE A WIDER RANGE OF TOOLS AND PLATFORMS. TWO YEARS BACK, EMAIL MARKETING DOMINATED AS THE CHANNEL THEY FOUND THE MOST EFFECTIVE (58%) FOLLOWED BY DEVELOPING THEIR CORPORATE WEBSITE (36%) AND CONTENT MARKETING (35%).

Fast-forward to today and content marketing has dramatically leapfrogged email marketing (email dropped from 58-41%) and the scores for online video and podcasts are 2.5 times higher (35%). Interestingly, despite Bigland's belief that social media isn't a key sales driver, it is still viewed as an effective channel by 39% of respondents

Customer Focus

Ultimately, all attendees agreed that the work that goes into adapting to new channels and measuring performance is a means to an end: focusing on the customer. For Tessian's Trehan, it isn't just important – it's a key driver of business. "Customer experience is really important. Everything we do is down to word-of-mouth." Survey respondents agree with the sentiment of executives around the table. A minority (18%) say customer experience is barely embedded, or not embedded at all, while it is increasing in importance for the vast majority (74%). Emma Raw, assistant director of digital marketing at EY, added: "It is now becoming a core focus. There has been an attitude (in B2B) that you're speaking to a business and not a person. We need to think of these businesses as people." Marketing can help with setting customer expectations that impact customer experience.

Skill Shortage

It's all very well to say B2B marketers should be working with all the tools available but, like in the past, finding marketers with the skills to either use technologies or operate in a B2B culture is still a challenge – one of the other reasons for me to write this book.

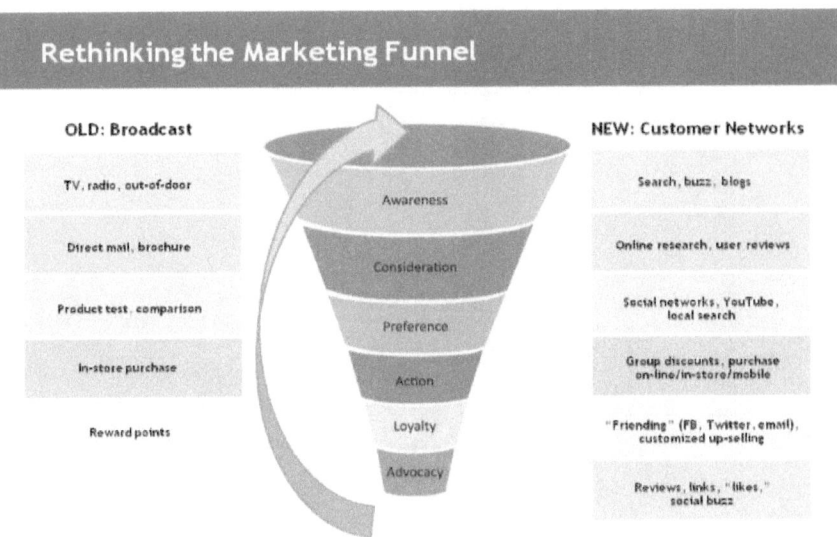

From "The Network Is Your Customer," by David Rogers

Traditional Marketing	Modern Marketing
• Marketing needs to interrupt the customer to get attention	• Customers control their attention and marketers engage when and how consumers want
• Marketing pushes a "consistent" message to the marketplace	• Marketers join the conversation by enabling communities of customers, prospects, partners, and other influencers
• Limited set of marketing channels	• Rapid proliferation of (and experimentation with) new measurable and targetable channels
• Marketing is mostly right-brained (creativity and art)	• Marketing is mostly left-brained (science and math)
• Marketers are not held fully accountable and (as a result) are not considered strategic at many organizations	• Marketers can demonstrate bottom-line impact, justify their budget, and plan the marketing mix with quantitative rigor

Is digital selling or marketing the only way? Or can influencer branding help nurture trusty customers in the form of thought leadership? In B2B, becoming a thought leader is a given, to ensure growth and sustainability.

BUILDING A BRAND WITH B2B MARKETING TRENDS

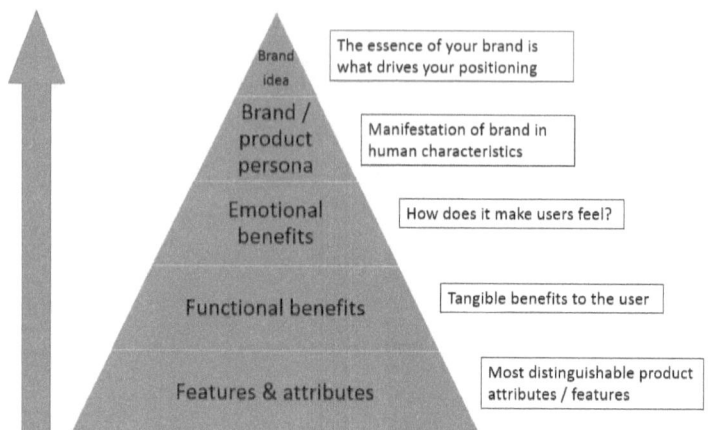

Hone Your Story: People and businesses like to feel personally connected with whom they are engaging. They want to know your story. They want to understand your company's values. As we had discussed in the section on digital selling, podcasts and success stories are a great way for them to feel connected and uplift like-minded businesses. Quality content makes your business feel more approachable, which generates higher conversion rates. Adopt B2C tactics and tell your story but you would be wise to avoid unnecessary technical jargon in favor of succinctly telling your customers what your core beliefs and value include, and how you can help them. Every engagement you make is an opportunity to sell your brand, but it is key to keep it light and fresh. The goal is to come across as an approachable brand which produces content that resonates with the audience and adds value by educating them on your business. You want to come across as a trustworthy brand with business transparency.

Content Marketing – Informed and Opinionated: Content marketing is nothing new, but it is an invaluable tool that every B2B marketing professional should have in their arsenal. Whether it is via blogs, videos, or podcasts, content marketing is a tried, tested, and successful marketing trend. Being an influencer or a thought leader in your space translates to authority which, in turn, translates to a better ROI of your marketing budget. B2C methodologies are slowly being adopted in the B2B content marketing landscape. Perhaps, the greatest benefit of content marketing is that you can turn your audience into volunteer marketers through word-of-mouth, sharing, and reposting content that ultimately extends your reach by creating a palpable buzz within your industry. One of the best ways to leverage your content marketing efforts is by creating educational content about your industry. This promotes your brand as a thought leader and provides immediate value to your audience – this can be done in the form of blogs, videos, guides, tutorials, and informational social media posts. Remember – consistency is key! If you want to maximize customer retention and maintain an attentive audience, then you need to deliver timely, relevant, and valuable content on a regular schedule. Keep your content fresh, upbeat and unique.

Thought Leadership – Brand Champions Crucial to B2B Marketing Success

Stepping into a new role where digital platforms, artificial intelligence, and analytics need to be leveraged to succeed in B2B marketing is intimidating. Marketers are trying to catch up with the digital buyer to win, serve, and retain. Marketers are borrowing tools from B2C marketing to create engagement strategies that will guide potential customers through their digital buying journey. To ideally serve digital buyers, experts and leaders as well as sellers need to assume thought leader roles so that it encompasses transactional and digital selling in addition to vetting and setting appointments with customers. Consider aligning digital sellers to key phases of the buyer journey and create specific roles for nurturing, outreach and sales. When you leverage thought leaders to deepen customer relationships and raising brand awareness, identifying how your brand brings the business strategy to life becomes a tad easier; by helping your customers understand what you have to offer through strategy playbooks and roadmaps.

Account-based Marketing (ABM)

Account-based marketing is a hyper-targeted approach that identifies existing customers or customers who are aware of your service and then directs marketing efforts towards them. ABM is often overlooked but it works because it cuts down on your marketing budget and eliminates time and energy wastage that was spent in generating leads when it could be used more effectively to nurture existing relationships. It is a high performing marketing channel that takes the traditional marketing funnel and flips it on its head as shown in the diagram below.

92% of B2B marketers cite ABM as extremely important to their overall marketing efforts

Traditional Marketing   Account-Based Marketing

While ABM has been around for over a decade, businesses have started to realize its full potential only now – the potential for delivering highly personalized and relevant campaigns to their target audience.

Where ABM Meets Thought Leadership

Identify a list of target accounts – where you'd have to tailor campaigns to specific accounts by finding accounts that match your ideal target customer – this will narrow down your focus area to what business companies will want to do with you in future.

Research each account – in most cases, information will be available in the public domain and on the company website, press releases, and annual reports. Start with:

- **Market:** industry, company size, competition
- **Company:** revenue, market share, history, and legacy
- **Relationships:** organizational structure, buying teams

Create relevant content – B2B buyers like personalized content. The more personal and relevant it is, the higher the odds of a buyer engaging with you. Catalogue blog posts, case studies, white papers, and e-books for your ideal target customer. Also, for inspiration you could ask them questions such as: why they are looking for a new solution, how they shortlist vendors, and how they go about testing products and services. More on content marketing as a part of thought leadership marketing is discussed later in chapter 7.

Look for Brand Advocates

Once you have done your research and identified key accounts, look for individuals you think might work as brand advocates or thought leaders. Smart, good-quality thought leadership can create deeper relationships with your clients. These executives are most likely to award business to brands that share good thought leadership. The organizations that nail this mostly focus on getting the solutions in place to drive an account-based strategy at scale. For thought leadership-producing marketing teams, the benefit of an account-based approach is that the client-facing individual looks great when they showcase their expertise and it makes them valuable allies in the long run. When your thought leadership content is on-point, you can further use sales intelligence to distribute wisdom to the right people at the right stage in their buyer journey. Automation tools such as Pardot and Marketo can help bring your marketing communications under one umbrella. Syncing these tools with the sales CRM will help track your progress and activities and tweak your ABM approaches over time.

BE A TRUSTED ADVISOR AND UNDERSTAND WHAT YOUR STAKEHOLDERS BELIEVE. ARTICULATE A WELL-INFORMED POINT OF VIEW AND MAKE A STRONG CASE. PERSONALIZE THE MESSAGE FOR EVERY INDIVIDUAL WITHIN AN ACCOUNT. BY DOING THIS, YOU INSTILL CONFIDENCE, IMPROVE OUTREACH, AND QUADRUPLE THE VALUE.

When buyers understand the value being offered, they develop a strong emotional connect with your brand. This emotion will lead to brand loyalty. The emotional level between brands and customers plays a very important role in B2B marketing. A useful tool that can help you define the success of your brand is: a brand pyramid. It represents the customer loyalty and we will see more about this in the next chapter.

Garnering Loyalty at the Topmost Level with Thought Leadership

The brand pyramid below according to **Curata** helps marketers improve their focus, increase production by making better use of valuable resources, and create a steady supply of successful content.

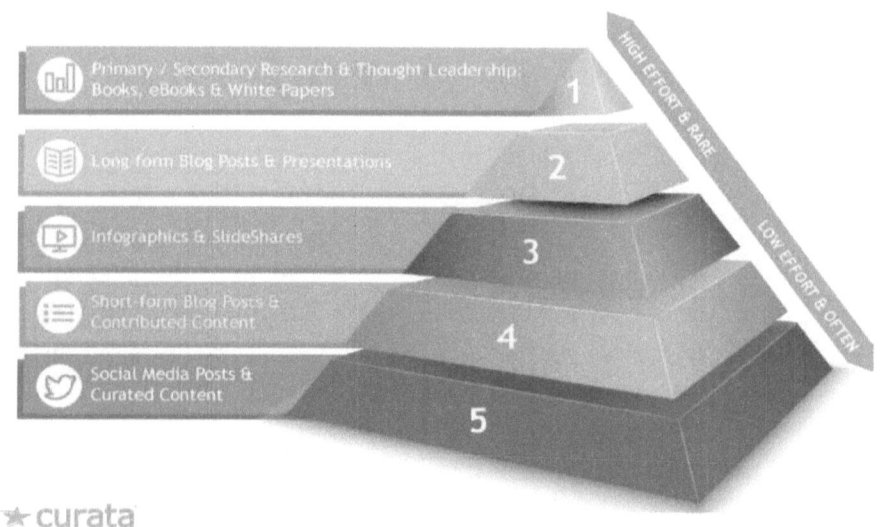

Source (Curata)

The topmost level of the pyramid represents core content for the most loyal customers. Content at this level represents meaningful research and insights. Use this research to create assets for thought leadership. These thought leadership pieces can be produced in the form of eBooks, guides, and printed material that give your customers an in-depth tour of the material. All the remaining assets as you descend the pyramid are usually gated content and are used to drive customers to the core asset of thought leadership and capture a lead. Once you have drilled down on your core content at the top that comprises thought leadership, you can begin to thread the needle for your organization's bigger goals that include brand awareness, lead generation, and digital sales.

PART II

EMERGENCE OF THOUGHT LEADERSHIP MARKETING

What is Thought Leadership Marketing?

THOUGHT LEADERSHIP – AN ART BEYOND JUST CONTENT MARKETING

In a nutshell, it is the positioning of your company as a leader in its field of expertise through blue-chip content that can take the form of articles, videos, podcasts, and research – but, what does this do exactly? Any form of original content that serves as an eye-opener to a problem in a niche, circulated within your industry or with potential clients may influence people to associate your brand with insight, expertise, and authority. When the time comes to hire a company for said expertise, you'd be at the top of their list.

CONTENT AND THOUGHT LEADERSHIP HAVE TO BE IN CAHOOTS ABOUT HOW THEY WORK TOGETHER – REMEMBER, CONTENT MARKETING AND THOUGHT LEADERSHIP AREN'T THE SAME. THOUGH THEY HAVE TO WORK IN UNISON FOR THE SAME GOAL.

Again, content marketing alone is just the creation and sharing of online content through blogs, social media posts, and videos. It doesn't explicitly contribute to brand promotion, but it is intended to stimulate interest among customers. You would have heard the phrase "content is king." For many B2B marketers, content marketing and thought leadership marketing are the same. Truth be told, they aren't. Content without context is just noise. Building thought leadership is about creating valuable, engaging content that builds trust and confidence with your customers, while content marketing focuses on churning out content continuously. However, the two are inter-dependent in a way.

ONE THING CONTENT AND THOUGHT LEADERSHIP MARKETING HAVE IN COMMON IS THAT THEY ARE BOTH CENTRAL TO CONTENT CREATION – BUT THE LATTER FOCUSES ON CRAFTING IMPACTFUL IDEAS AND NOT ON INCREASING REACH. THOUGHT LEADERSHIP CANNOT BE OUTSOURCED; IT MUST COME FROM WITHIN.

Beyond content marketing (that addresses immediate needs), thought leadership when used as a long-term strategy is a game changer. Content marketing serves the medium whereas thought leadership marketing serves the outcome – in relation to the bigger marketing picture. Even though content marketing is vital for customer engagement, establishing thought leadership helps portray your brand as an industry leader and innovator, and builds confidence with your audience. Thought leadership isn't an elevator pitch. Producing unnecessary content repeatedly has a downside – it will alienate your audience. Thought leadership content is your doorway to presenting your solutions within the purview of your product's capabilities. If you are a thought leader, the good news is that you don't have to be a perfectionist – just need to have a mindset of being capable to connect the dots in ways other people can't and the commitment to share your knowledge with industry peers.

Content Marketing – An Integral Part of Building Thought Leadership

Content Marketing vs Thought Leadership Marketing

Chances are, if you've been working in the B2B marketing space for a while, you probably have noticed that both content marketing and thought leadership have grown massively in popularity in recent years. However, there is a good deal of overlap between the two, so naturally there is room for confusion. Many have stepped into the breach to help describe the differences – here are a few I've come across:

"Thought leadership is the goal, content marketing is the means"

"Thought leadership is your belief/values, content marketing is the way you amplify the former"

"The distinction between thought leadership marketing and content marketing is genre vs style"

"Thought leadership and content marketing are like apple and oats. They go well together as they are both foods, but that's the end of it"

One significant problem with all the above statements is that they don't help in deciding where to apply one as compared to the other. If the first definition is 100% accurate, we don't need to invest any time and effort in thought leadership – we should just market good quality content until we attain a level of thought leadership in the industry. If the second one is true, we already have thought leadership, so all we need is effective content marketing till everyone knows what the brand stands for. The last two, though grandiose, yield no guidance whatsoever. However, from the above four definitions, it is reasonably clear how the two relate. Content marketing is a subset of thought leadership marketing – it does everything to position the firm as a leading expert in the field. As we pointed out in a previous chapter, a useful abridgement of content marketing is an approach to create and distribute content to attract and retain an audience and get them to spend money.

Content marketing predominantly includes the five pillars, i.e. plan, create, optimize, distribute, and analyze. It is a purely market-driven exercise aimed at advertising based on what consumers respond to. The subtle difference in execution between content marketing and thought leadership marketing is that the latter cannot be outsourced or just "churned out". It needs to come from an individual who is an authoritative voice in his industry. There is a vast middle-ground where thought leadership marketing and content marketing are intertwined. The key is to include authentic thought leadership in your content marketing strategy. To churn a high volume of quality thought leadership pieces, you need:

1. **Content experts** – using a combination of in-house and agency resources

2. **Management buy-in** – company executives should formulate thought leadership content. This requires educating your leadership on sharing their perspectives over various channels

---

Gaining customers' trust isn't an elusive quality – you either have it or you don't. Trust is a pragmatic, tangible, actionable asset that you can create

– Stephen Covey

Authentic thought leadership content is extremely valuable because it builds trust with your customers and eliminates risk from the buying process. Eliminate the risk and you build your buyers' confidence – they realize you know what you are doing. In 2013, Laura Ramos (Forrester) summarized the relationship between thought leadership and content marketing in a nice way.

THOUGHT LEADERSHIP SITS AT THE PINNACLE OF CONTENT MARKETING

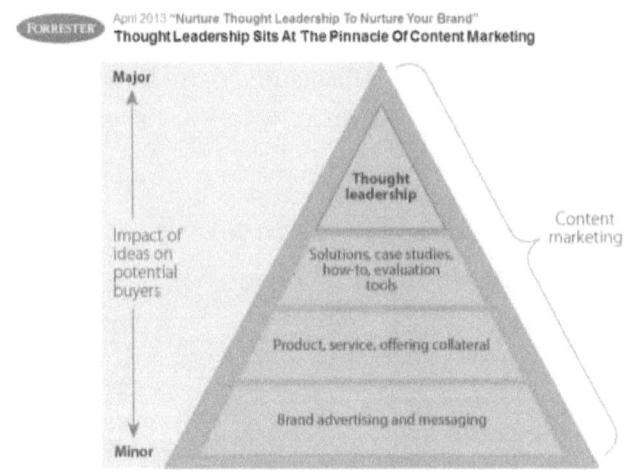

From the above diagram, we can see that thought leadership sits atop the pyramid because it is produced in lower volumes than other content – it is the toughest kind of content to create and market. It's focused on a few issues a firm should own; if done well, it has a great impact on a potential buyer, addressing his most vexing problems with a firm's best insights.

If thought leadership marketing is harder than content marketing, when do we deploy it?

- If customers are grappling with a significant problem or emerging trend in their industry
- Your firm has a better way to address the problem (or opportunity) or you can develop an opportunity through original research
- Your competitors do not have an assailable position in the same space

---

PERHAPS, THE BEST WAY TO THINK ABOUT THOUGHT LEADERSHIP MARKETING IS: AS A COMPONENT OF CONTENT MARKETING – ITSELF A COMPONENT OF THE OVERALL MARKETING MIX. THE RECIPE COMPRISING THE TWO SHOULD BE DISTINGUISHABLE, OR THE AFTERMATH WOULD BE A LUMPY AND UNAPPETIZING GOOP

There are many real-world examples of excellent B2B thought leadership content. When done well, it can provoke a reaction from consumers eagerly looking for information – the kind of information people are willing to consume and share with their peers. Let's look at a couple of examples.

Example 1 – Philips Future Health Index

Source: Philips Health Index Stories

Philips, an Amsterdam-based company, is a well-known manufacturer of home electronics. With close to 130 years of history behind them, they have grown to be one of the largest electronics companies in the world. What you may not be aware of, is that Philips is currently focusing on healthcare and lighting. The Philips website has a microsite named Our Future Health Index Stories. They believe in using intelligible data to deliver better health outcomes and healthcare business solutions. Philips uses this microsite to position themselves as an advanced healthcare technology company and leader. The Future Health Index is a think tank of healthcare leaders and advisors focused on creating a supportable healthcare system for the future. It has several blogs, articles, and videos that leverage artificial intelligence, patient data, health economics, and much more. These pieces on innovative solutions are a great example of effective thought leadership content because they address actual challenges of user experience in clinical scenarios around the world from a patient's standpoint and from a healthcare provider's standpoint.

Philips presents information on digital health (consumer health and patient data), products, solutions, and several other industry-related topics in a variety of formats from blogs, narrative feature stories to data-driven case studies and news articles presented in highly shareable formats.

Example 2 – Johnson and Johnson

Another multi-national corporation founded over 100 years ago – Johnson and Johnson develops medical devices, pharmaceutical and consumer packaged goods. J&J has over 200 brands in its portfolio so getting people excited about what they have on offer is a major challenge. They create top-notch thought leadership content by crafting messages for both consumers and businesses alike.

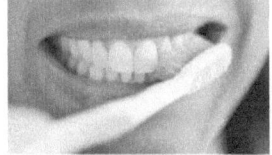

February 24, 2020

Could the Answer to Preventing Hospital-Acquired Pneumonia Be as Simple as Better Oral Care? This Nurse Thinks So

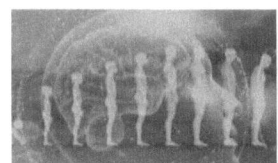

January 06, 2020

The Quest for "Immorbidity": What If You Could Live a Long Life—Disease-Free?

January 01, 2020

"I Have a Vision for Helping Advance Healthcare": Meet 6 Leaders Working on Inspiring Innovations in 2020

December 15, 2019

A Year of Firsts: 6 Ways Johnson & Johnson Made History in 2019

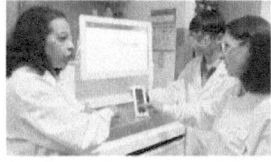

December 02, 2019

Have IBD? Read About the Next Frontier in Disease Research That Taps Into the Microbiome

October 17, 2019

The Man Behind the Brands You Use Every Day: 6 Questions for Johnson & Johnson's Head of Consumer Health

For example: an article on 7 simple winter beauty hacks showcases expert-approved tips by Dr. Tina Alster, M.D. who is a board-certified dermatologist in Washington D.C. and expert with the American Society for Dermatologic Surgery (ASDS). Or another example where Johnson &

Johnson showcased their ground-breaking research in an in-depth article about autism, the power of human-centered healthcare technology, or a story about developing a vaccine to fight against the Zika virus by famed Brazilian scientist Dr. Leda Castilho, Ph.D. – all cutting-edge research content that focuses on real-world scenarios with real-world industry experts. This added a great deal of value to J&J's repertoire as a thought leader and industry expert in medical research and cosmetic business solutions. Their content presentation is excellent. Ranging from eBooks and podcasts to whitepapers and interviews, they know how to leave a lasting impression on a consumer.

Example 3 – Burning Glass Technologies

Burning Glass Technologies is a for-profit enterprise that generates knowledge about labor and the job market. It stands toe-to-toe with trusted voices like the Bureau of Labor Statistics through its deep trove of fresh, formidable data. For its thought leadership content, it synthesizes all that raw info into job market analytics and reports like Saving the Associates of Arts Degree.

Source (BluLeadz, n.d.)

Example 4 – Build a Better Agency

Source (BluLeadz, n.d.)

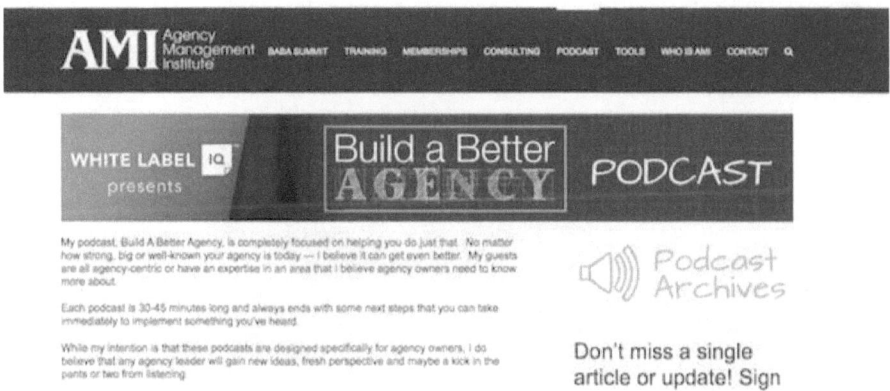

Drew McLellan is a well-known name in the world of digital marketing who has pioneered a wide range of high-impact approaches to getting your message heard. His 'Build a Better Agency' podcast is an example of structuring thought leadership content creatively in a way that appeals to the preferences and the needs of his audience – in this case, time-strapped agency leaders.

Example 5 – IBM Watson Marketing

Source (BluLeadz, n.d.)

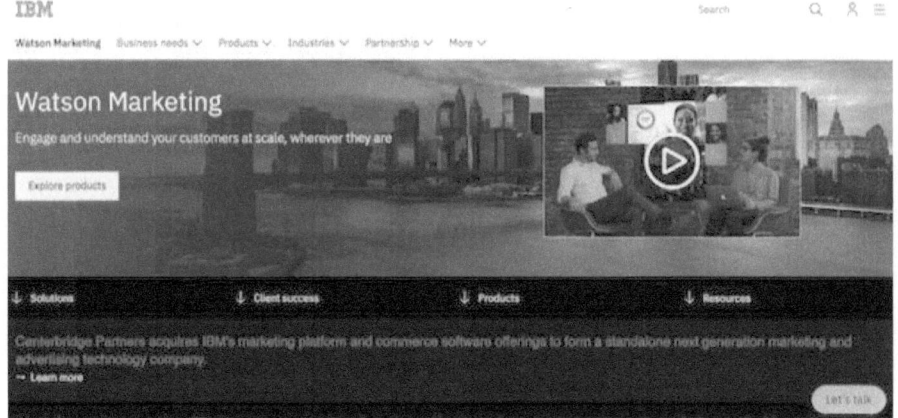

IBM's THINK Marketing platform is built on one of the most visible emblems of its thought leadership credentials: The AI "supercomputer" Watson. Watson analyzes individual web users in real-time on a level that most digital marketers can only dream of. Then, it renders an ultra-personalized experience where customization itself demonstrates the company's excellence.

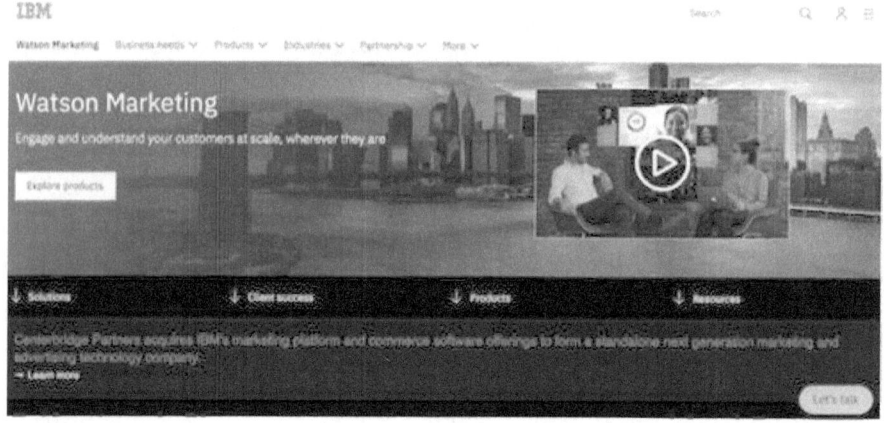

When it comes to brand advocacy and authenticity, the stakes are high with companies today. Authenticity garners loyalty. Nurturing loyalty is imperative to attracting buyers and loyalty nurtured is a customer closed.

Thought Leadership to Capture, Convince, Close

Creating quality content plays a critical role in ensuring the success of your thought leadership strategy. Using listicles and videos are great too – with a lot of examples and quotes from industry leaders. A well-positioned thought leadership strategy with sound content marketing reinforces trust, awareness, and long-term loyalty. I also love the idea of curating content from other sources while adding my own perspective. Your audience is looking for help. Are you willing to give it to them? To ideate a strategy that effectively accomplishes your goal and builds your influence, the following three points are crucial.

Building Trust – With No Strings Attached!

Every business has an agenda, and your audience knows that. Exceed your customers' expectations by giving them something in return for nothing. By sharing your insights and expertise with your audience, you're giving them a reason to trust you. When you let go of the need to promote yourself and your company, and focus on providing actual, real-life value to the people who matter the most, you'll earn their trust. So, focus on educating your audience by giving them valuable information about topics they're interested in. When the content teaches your customers something useful, helps solve a problem, or simply entertains them, they'll be motivated to keep an eye out for your future content. People are skeptical, don't waste valuable time explaining why they should trust you. Just show them.

Preparing Content for Specific Milestones

Once you have figured out your content's role in building trust, you need to create specific kinds of content for specific points throughout your relationship with a potential lead. Writing guest thought leader posts for your audience is a great start. Once you have their attention, keep it engaging through insightful blog posts, case studies, and videos – anything that reinforces your position as a trusted expert. Leverage your social media accounts and email newsletter campaigns to deliver the right content in a timely manner.

THOUGHT LEADERSHIP CONTENT IS LESS ABOUT QUANTITY AND MORE ABOUT QUALITY - HOW WELL YOU USE IT OVER TIME TO KEEP YOUR AUDIENCES ENGAGED.

Building an Online Presence

You've put in the effort to craft good content, but your job isn't finished. Collaborate with contacts in your network and share relevant pieces with those who can benefit. Surround your brand with high-quality messaging and create an online presence that others in your industry can't ignore (especially when they're actively seeking out more information). Utilize and repurpose your content constantly in other creative ways such as a speaking engagement, guest on a podcast, etc.

A "one size fits all" approach doesn't work for thought leadership. However, I believe in 3 crucial tenets to kickstart your thought leadership strategy that I've aptly phrased as the 3 'C's of thought leadership.

THE 3 'C's OF THOUGHT LEADERSHIP

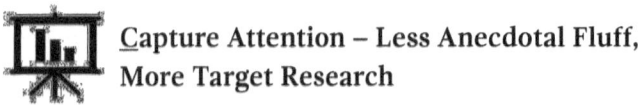 **Capture Attention – Less Anecdotal Fluff, More Target Research**

Companies need to pay special attention to customer concerns and business needs. How you engage with your customers while solving a problem for them will ultimately decide how your expertise is received. Don't try to be the jack of all trades. Focusing on one specific niche is much more viable for faster growth. The more granular the research, the more faith you will have in your thought leadership strategy. You want to present a dearth of valuable knowledge to your audience that no one else in your industry can provide while also defining your customers' challenges and ways to overcome them.

Deloitte Insights is a great example of an organization that has done extensive research in different fields to position itself as a thought leader for knowledge. Deloitte is a professional services company that specializes in consulting and auditing. They work with many industries from technological firms to government organizations and many more. What really stands out for Deloitte as their USP is that they have a wealth of knowledge and expertise at their disposal. Which is why curating useful, high quality content for a specific target audience sits at the core of their marketing mission. Deloitte produces content in a variety of formats from webcasts to podcasts, blogs, and more. They have a little bit for everyone who wants to learn about them and the industries they cater to.

So, what can we learn from Deloitte? Target research is vital right? Creating quality content would be very challenging especially when you're trying to develop a messaging that must traverse a massive target audience like Deloitte's. If you have a look at their website, you will see that they have several specialties that are segregated by topic, sector, and by spotlight. But what makes them a great source of information and a thought leader is that they create discoverable, navigable content microsites for every niche that functions as a hub for target audiences of various groupings.

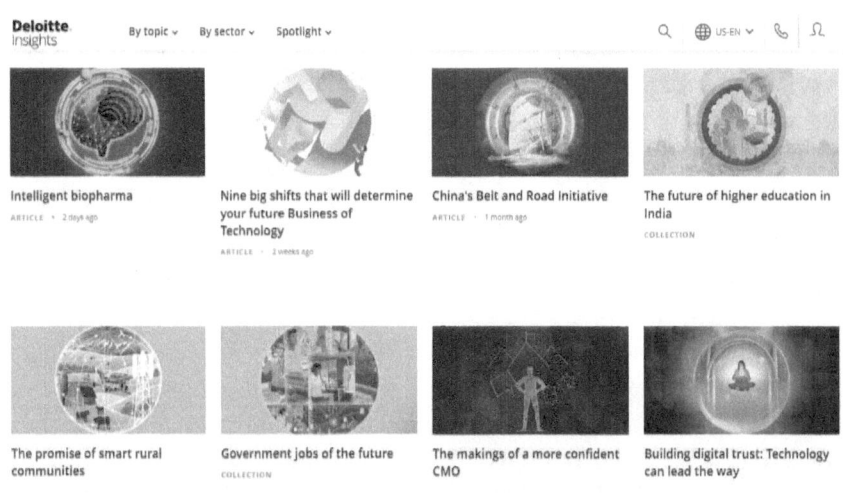

Avoid the gimmick of product showboating – your audience will sense this right at the start and probably tune out leading to a major loss in the trust you tried so hard to nurture. Which comes back to research: companies need to conduct thorough research of their target audience. In some rare cases it may not be in a very specific niche yet, so it pays to have a general notion of what your topic entails. This could include:

- Research to find a well-founded source. Scour the internet – social media platforms such as Twitter, Quora, and LinkedIn will have a fair number of topics doing the rounds for B2B audiences.
- Keep a questionnaire for yourself. For your customers: a few questions initially and then some more to follow up to ensure the conversation moves smoothly in your favor.
- Being specific is key. This is vital for creating nuanced content to make it as engaging as possible for your customer. Look for real-life instances so that you can reaffirm your views through these examples.

Insights From Surveys

You and your company need to focus on creating original research to get through to customers and change their perception of the value you are trying to offer. Investing the time for market research of your target audience that focuses on customer needs and sales will pay off with a strong strategy in place. The objective here is to procure research from across the organization as the starting point of all the ideas you want to build upon and deliver to customers. Document all existing market research, guidelines, and sales information in one repository. Then brainstorm with several industry experts on these areas and develop many different topics that could drive the company's sales. This list of topics could be the basis of a strategy that might yield ideas of which area the company wants to be a credible authority in. Once you have narrowed down to a topic/theme, conduct surveys.

INSIGHTS FOUNDED THROUGH RESEARCH OF YOUR TARGET AUDIENCE CAN HELP YOUR BRAND STAND OUT AND ESTABLISH YOUR STANCE AS A THOUGHT LEADER.

Make sure the takeaways of your survey are closely aligned with the buy-ins of your business and sales stakeholders. They play an important role in bringing the insights from surveys to the fore in order to initiate conversations with your potential customers. You need to have a dedicated team in place for this entire process – from narrowing down on topics to potential leads from content assets you created and shared. Finally, revisiting the second point stated above, keep a well-prepared questionnaire ready. Some of the points that need to be addressed while researching your target audience can be as follows:

1. What survey instrument is being used?
2. What is the customer's pain points in the survey the company needs to address?
3. What is the survey's purpose? What issues are being addressed?
4. Can the company provide any solutions based on insights received from the surveys?
5. What channels should be used to optimize the market spend for the solution?
6. Make use of influencer marketing software to manage brand advocates on a unified platform

Once your target audience is ready to fill out the questionnaire through survey tools, in-person at a conference, or over the telephone, engage them meaningfully so they feel comfortable enough to answer your queries honestly. Upon completion, look over the responses you received and formulate key findings that could be aligned to your thought leadership strategy. These insights should be reiterated in the form of a research report along with supported reasoning for customers' opinions. The report could be created in the form of infographics, whitepapers, blogs, videos, and so on – anything that combines all your content assets in a deducible tone.

 **Close Prospects – An SME Ecosystem with the Right Messaging**

Connecting your brand message to the solution you are trying to sell

A powerful brand message is a vital component of a strong thought leadership strategy. Before you share your story with the world, it is important that you completely understand what your messaging stands for. Getting the right message positioning in your industry is all about communicating a consistent brand USP to customers and other stakeholders. You need to have a clear picture of the differentiating factors between your business and the rest of the market by analyzing:

- History of the brand and its legacy
- Goals that need to be achieved
- Culture of the company
- Niche or the industry being catered to
- Competitors in the same space

Each of the above five points is vital to improving visibility with your target audience. A well-worded message will convince customers to see you as an authoritative force with a compelling back story. Many organizations struggle in aligning their messaging with the solutions and services they offer. One way to improve your brand messaging is by creating marketing/sales playbooks and other proprietary assets to drive the value proposition deeper into the B2B buyer cycle and engage in day-to-day conversations. To create assets of value, companies need to invest time and money into onboarding SMEs who are authorities in their area of specialization. So, I think you get the gist. 'Thought leaders' and 'subject matter experts' are terms that are often thrown back and forth interchangeably. However, they are not the same. A thought leader is a seasoned SME by default, but the reverse may not always be true. SMEs have their own views and best practice approaches. The intent is right though – nurture and invest in hiring subject matter experts to help develop the understanding of your niche further. Having an SME ecosystem in place is the way to take your brand messaging forward. While at Wipro, I set up the Wipro Council for Industry Research which identified internal SMEs across business verticals who were nurtured through a systematic process to contribute to Wipro's thought leadership marketing journey.

DRIVING THOUGHT LEADERSHIP WITH SMEs: MOTIVATE YOUR SMEs BY BUILDING TRUST WITH THEM – THROUGH EMPATHY AND RESPECT

How should companies maintain an SME ecosystem like the research council stated above to improve their thought leadership content? There are always a few knowledge-rich subject matter experts in every organization. These experts could be:

Seasoned salespersons – These folks understand the 'revenue problem' better than most. They know the drivers behind why some of the company's business solutions need work and other factors B2B buyers might consider before making a purchase.

Customer service and experience – A team that has an encyclopedia of customer information ranging from customer satisfaction indexes to repeat-conversion barriers. They are the battlefront of customer churn reduction, and their ideas and insights can prove to be a very helpful asset in shaping thought leadership content that may ease a buyer's dilemma.

Last, but not the least.... excellent writers – Experts who can condense awfully long, technical information to something that can be consumed easily by the audience. These writers understand the importance of brevity and are also skilled at understanding the audience and capable of interviewing SMEs in the industry.

Leveraging Experts to Create a Better SME Ecosystem

SMEs are busy individuals. Chances are, they may not be entirely on board with supporting a thought leadership cause especially if they must devote a lot of time. On the off chance that their ideas are not completely aligned with the company's business goals and strategy, engage with them patiently. Ask them what they want to focus on. What do they feel are the most pressing customer concerns right now? Are there any new industry trends or regulations doing the rounds? Did their ideas influence a customer decision? The possibilities are endless. Furthermore, if you want your SMEs to contribute to any thought leadership content, you need to give very concise guidelines and clear real-world examples of what exactly you are looking for.

Consumer packaged goods (CPG) manufacturer Whole Foods is an apt example of a thought leader leveraging SMEs through content generation which is rare for a CPG manufacturer. They mix traditional CPG marketing with their content and storytelling by showing their shoppers reasons for repeat customers – a healthy and wholesome selection of produce and groceries.

Whole Foods also focused on local stores and promoted a 'greener' lifestyle by ridding their stores of plastic bags in 2008 – again, this has a great environmental message attached to it that would greatly influence and impress the general population to follow suit. Whole Foods partnered with Top Chef (an American reality television cooking competition) to promote their food. They got a great deal of exposure from Top Chef as the contestants on the show used Whole Foods' ingredients. It was a win-win for both parties since there was no money involved and Top Chef viewers were Whole Foods' customers and vice-versa.

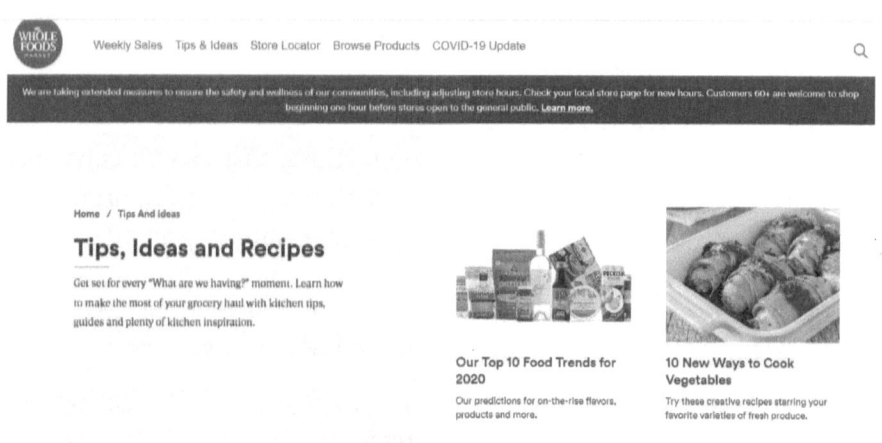

Another excellent example of leveraging SMEs to close customers with thought leadership is the partnership between Mind Your Own Business or MYOB (a provider of business solutions in Australia and New Zealand) and finance experts to manage the finances of various organizations.

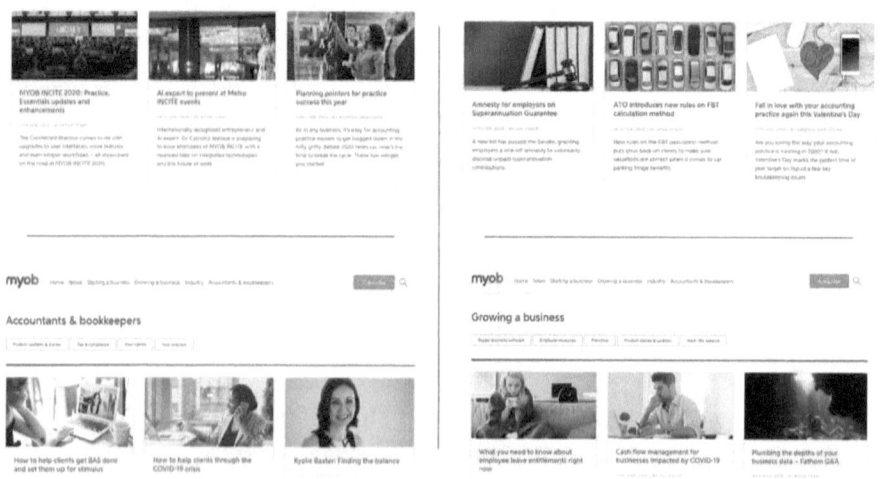

What MYOB does is: they help companies manage their funds by connecting them with bookkeepers and finance professionals. They mostly cater to small businesses and a few established organizations too. MYOB creates a unique content strategy for each challenge it faces and provides the resources and expertise to navigate each business problem.

You, as a representative of your brand, need to sit down and interview your SMEs to develop your thought leadership content, understand that these experts want a chance to communicate their ideas and experiences in a manner that reflects on their best practices that will enhance their reputation in the industry. Set the agenda for your discussions upfront so every attendee understands what must be achieved within the stipulated time. Multiple SMEs in the same room will want to get his/her point across; so, it is very important to ensure that there are no distractive tangents that might cause the discussion to stray from the topic at hand. Do your due diligence beforehand. Don't be afraid to probe and frame questions a little differently if you feel you aren't getting the right answers. Subject matter expertise is a goldmine. Just depends on how deep you are willing to dig. Leveraging SME partners to broadcast your brand message will greatly improve your reputation within the industry and improve your organic search engine rankings and reach.

Finally, once you have successfully completed your thought leadership content, don't forget to say thanks. Share your published work with them – it makes them feel good. Success helps create loyalty and future cooperation.

 Convince – Improve Conversions with a Great Lead Nurture Strategy

How important is it for companies to leverage top-quality content in lead nurturing to help convert prospects into satisfied customers? Very! Any prospects attracted by your content online will continue to be interested in useful information as the selling cycle progresses.

Some of the best tips for using content in your lead nurturing stage of the marketing funnel to turn curious leads into satisfied customers are as follows:

In-depth Information and Resources – As B2B buyers shift from the awareness stage of the buyer journey to the decision stage, their thirst for valuable information increases. Your lead-nurturing strategy should include multiple messaging formats that delve deeper than what you would normally provide at the lead nurturing stage. These formats could be:

Research Reports and Webinars – When narrowing down on a solution or product in a niche, buyers get influenced by data and statistics that reinforce the need for a fix and some possible best practice pointers. Sharing original research would go a long way to improve your chances of establishing thought leadership. Webinars, on the other hand, are great for outlining common issues that could get solved with the solution you are offering. A B2B buyer participates in webinars mostly when he/she senses a significant problem and is looking for an effective remedy.

For example, the following stats will give you some idea into why nurturing leads is important for thought leadership content.

- *49% of B2B buyers said their opinion of a company deteriorated after reading poor quality content, and one-third had removed a company from consideration based on its thought leadership output. (Edelman 2020 B2B thought leadership impact study)*
- *35% of B2B buyers spend 1-3 hours per week reviewing thought leadership content. (Edelman 2020 B2B thought leadership impact study)*
- *A company's authenticity is directly related to the likelihood that customers become advocates for that brand. Authentic brands attract high-value customers. (Edelman 2020 B2B thought leadership impact study)*
- *About 50% of B2B marketers believe thought leadership builds trust in an organization. Among actual buyers, that number is around 83%. (Edelman 2020 B2B thought leadership impact study)*

Case Studies – During lead nurturing, once a buyer realizes that a solution to their problem exists, they need evidence to support their conclusion. Furnishing proof displaces skepticism and helps shift the buyer's focus away from hesitation. Any case studies that highlight how your solution solved a problem for a company is gold. Buyers want to know that your solution has indeed helped other brands with their hurdles.

Lead nurturing is a powerful way to engage with a future buyer. Shifting from lead generation to lead nurturing in your funnel entails showing customers your credibility through various means and offering a relevant, timely solution. The right type of content in lead nurturing is as important as delivering great content for lead generation.

Podcasts – Personalized podcasts are often a much more interactive experience for intrigued customers. Embedding videos in company websites is a standard practice nowadays. As a thought leader, one can offer better, impactful insights, share success stories, instill a sense of urgency among customers to sit up, listen, and act.

To convince your target audience, look for leaders who answer 3 fundamental questions:

Do these "thought leaders" have deep subject matter expertise?

Generalism – podcast hosts steer clear of generalists, always! Having domain-specific knowledge is very important and being able to talk about a specific topic for an extended period is often a mandate.

Is this person known and respected in the industry?

Having a good social media presence doesn't always translate to top-notch quality. Extensive due diligence to check if the thought leader indeed has deep expertise on the subject matter is often preferred over just a good number of followers on Twitter.

What differentiates this 'thought leader' from all the others?

The best in the business are always up to date on current trends and subjects. They are excellent communicators, build great relationships, and are altruistic. They like to serve their community with value and are willing to share their knowledge and expertise.

Leveraging Digital Mediums The Way Forward

The fact is, change is coming. Leveraging digital mediums effectively to spread your brand's message is the way forward. Being a thought leader and marketing with complete transparency and expertise goes a long way in establishing credibility with your audience. It is a much more reliable way to get customers to buy your products or services once you have them convinced.

Thought leadership requires content to convert customers, but all the content in the world won't guarantee you thought leadership. Instead, you need a strategy tailored to your specific goal. Start by crafting each piece of content with an unwavering purpose in mind until you have the individual building blocks of your strategy. Then, assemble them in such a way that they work together, yielding a total that is more than just the sum of its parts. How businesses connect with customers at each stage of the relationship lifecycle is very important – you need to focus on personalization at every juncture of customer engagement. Tailor-made initiatives on B2B buyers' industry roles and business challenges give buyers the liberty to engage on their own terms depending on their preferred channel of engagement.

**BUYERS NEED OUR IDEAS TO DRIVE INNOVATION
AND THRIVE IN A CONNECTED ECONOMY.**

My 5F Model: Build and Implement a Successful Thought Leadership Marketing Program

Thought leadership is a powerful and challenging mountain to climb. Some might argue that overuse of the term has reduced it to jargon, but the value of thought leadership when done effectively is anything but useless. In fact, authentic thought leadership remains a driving force behind successful companies across industries. The future of thought leadership is bright, but it's not without flaws. For every leader that builds and executes a solid thought leadership strategy, quite a few take a potshot at it and miss. It's never about having an 'x' number of followers. It is a continuous process of educating and building trust with your audience members through high-quality content that engages them. We believe, even the best content needs a driver and direction. Brands often make the mistake of thinking that any content, if it's 'good enough', will help them accomplish their marketing goals. Too many strategies fail to coalesce a brand's content assets together effectively.

ALL YOUR CONTENT – GUEST POSTS, BLOGS, PRESS MENTIONS, WHITEPAPERS SHOULD WORK TOGETHER TO BRING YOU CLOSER TO YOUR THOUGHT LEADERSHIP GOAL. MISALIGNED STRATEGIES THAT DON'T ENSURE ALL ASSETS WORK HARMONIOUSLY WOULD CREATE THOUGHT LEADERS WITH LOTS OF CONTENT AND LITTLE INFLUENCE TO SHOW FOR IT.

Which is why I developed the **5F framework** to help organizations position themselves as thought leaders in the minds of their clients. This model has been successfully deployed for our clients and has shown them amazing results.

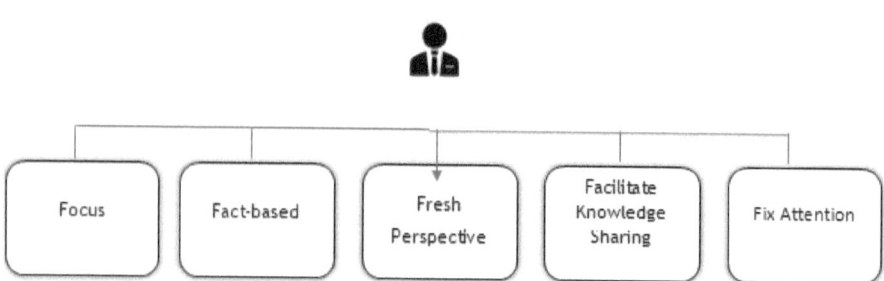

Focus...on the Customer!

Good thought leadership gets to the crux of the issue of what keeps your clients awake at night. If your content provokes very little interest from them, it may be focusing too much on your firm's offering, and not enough on your clients' problems. And it's not just about today's problems. Your insights and thought leadership content should also help clients make sense of the future. Keeping on top of emerging trends is executives' number one reason for reading about thought leadership (as identified by 66% of respondents in a Grist survey which we will talk about in chapter 15). It's important to understand industry perspective, trends, content topics customers consume, content formats they prefer, and channels that consume this content. Added to this complexity is the number of decision-makers involved in the buying process and the customized content they demand. Mapping this is important to ensure you are offering content they would like to consume and not pushing content that you think is important for them.

Fact-based Approach

Research forms the core of any thought leadership marketing campaign. Companies should leverage primary and secondary research to gain insights and data on potential trends, which can add to the foundation of the thought leadership marketing campaign. The next step is to identify the topic that is closely associated with your brand. Are you an authority on that topic? A simple Google search can help you answer that question. Often, we find that brands are not just competing with their direct competitors but with everyone else too. Anyone who publishes content in your space is competing for mind share and authority. You also need to identify the questions your customers are asking. Identify all of them, make a list and prioritize them. Then find the experts within your company who can answer them. Address these problems across multiple formats and platforms in a way that adds value to your audience. Start with the most important and work your way down the list. Finally, you need to create your thought leadership content in an engaging way.

Fresh Perspective

Having a unique perspective from the data gathered through research is the third step in the process. An expert partner can help companies arrive at a unique positioning for companies which can then be communicated consistently across all identified marketing channels. Thought leaders can shape the future trends of an organization and bring heightened levels confidence to the team and in-market while dealing with all the B2B challenges. Being open about the values and concerns and working towards bettering society can help build a long-lasting relationship with clients.

Facilitate Knowledge Sharing

Thought leaders should always look at sharing their knowledge and insights with a wider pool of stakeholders to ensure they are able to create a strong network of influencers that can act as ambassadors during any bidding process.

Fixed Attention

The final step is where you create attention capturing content (blogs, articles, point of views, white papers, infographics, videos, etc.) which consistently showcases your expertise and grabs your clients' attention and in turn helps capture market-share. Your content needs to be subtly aligned with the expertise you offer. You must avoid an explicit sales pitch, but there's little point in producing and researching startlingly original ideas if they don't align with your proposition. If you have to forcibly fuse your expert commentary into research findings, then you've got the wrong idea. It is not going to fulfill the purpose – no matter how great an idea it was. Think about your organization's niche and capabilities when choosing your thought leadership content themes. And get your client-facing teams involved early in the development process:

something a surprisingly low 42% of B2B firms currently do, according to research.

We have talked about the five Fs. So how do you achieve it? Easier said than done, right?

Well-crafted content can help you reach and grow your specific audience, build relationships with that audience at scale, and enhance your credibility as a leader and influencer in your space. But you can only accomplish these objectives when you develop each piece of content in accordance with a strategy that's aligned to your thought leadership goal. The best thought leadership strategies help you build and maintain trust with the audiences that are most valuable to you and your company. They do so by using a variety of content assets that work together to reach new audiences, engage them with valuable resources, and keep your brand on everyone's mind so that you're the first point of contact they think of when a need or opportunity arises.

ITSMA Thought Leadership Maturity Model

Continuing from 5F model for building thought leadership, let's look at two reports on thought leadership and B2B engagement created by ITSMA which was shared with me during my interview with Mr. Dave Munn - President and CEO, ITSMA. ITSMA (IT Service Marketing Association) is a leading marketing organization for technology, communications, and professional services who have been at the forefront of thought leadership marketing. They have been defining and building B2B services for 25 years The first report is called the ITSMA Thought Leadership Maturity Model prepared by (ITSMA, 2014) and the second one is titled: How Executives Engage prepared by (Julie Schwartz, Senior VP, ITSMA, 2018). You can visit ISMA's website to learn more about what they do, and read their whitepapers and case studies on engagement and brand advocacy. This chapter highlights why marketers and thought leaders need to focus on personalization at every step of the engagement lifecycle. In this study, we explore why we need to provide personalized solutions to B2B buyers, why content in multiple formats is vital, and how to handle the shift from face-to-face to digital experiences.

THE ITSMA THOUGHT LEADERSHIP MATURITY MODEL

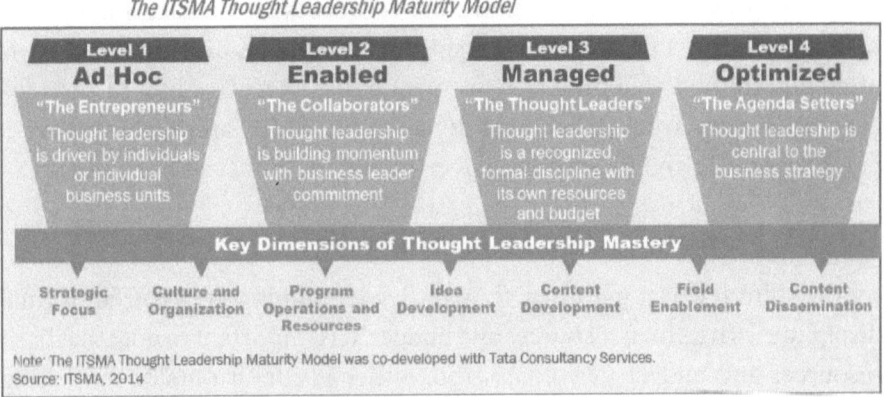

The ITSMA Thought Leadership Maturity Model

Note: The ITSMA Thought Leadership Maturity Model was co-developed with Tata Consultancy Services.
Source: ITSMA, 2014

The Four Levels of Thought Leadership Maturity

From the above figure, we can see four stages of maturity. Each level reflects a different degree of formalization, organizational coordination, and integration into the overall go-to-market approach. In principle, the higher the level of maturity, the greater the impact of the thought leadership program on the organization's reputation and the better the program's return on investment. Even so, the highest level of maturity does not necessarily have to be the best, or even achievable for every organization.

Level 1: Ad-hoc – The Entrepreneurs

At the first level, thought leadership is essentially driven by individual SMEs or business units. At this stage, thought leadership is typically loosely coordinated and not fully embedded in the organization's marketing and sales efforts. Funding is often limited to one-off projects and limited to a few communication channels. While there may be anecdotal evidence that thought leadership is beneficial, it has a limited impact because it isn't integrated into a broader marketing plan.

Level 2: Enabled – The Collaborators

At the second level of maturity, thought leadership is building momentum within the organization and has gained business leaders' commitment. This commitment is important because it helps ensure that thought leadership becomes more closely incorporated into the organization's go-to-market plan and sales methodology. With senior leaders in agreement, we get a formal approach to allocating resources and measuring results. Although there is greater sponsorship of thought leadership, funding is often determined on a project-by-project basis. Executive buy-in and idea generation vary from division to division, but SMEs are likely to have a personal profile and be externally recognized in their field of expertise.

Level 3: Managed – The Thought Leaders

By the third level of maturity, thought leadership is a recognized, formal discipline with its own resources and budget. It is important to note that both resources and budget may come from either inside or outside marketing or both. At this stage, there are formal, clearly defined processes in place to identify, develop, and manage thought leadership content; budgets to fund its creation; and an agreed-upon set of metrics by which to evaluate the impact of thought leadership. There is a corporate thought leadership program that coordinates across business units, but individual business units may still pursue some topics outside the corporate agenda. At this stage, SMEs are accountable for generating thought leadership material.

Level 4: Optimized – The Agenda Setters

At the highest level of maturity in the ITSMA model, thought leadership is not only fully incorporated into the organization's marketing and sales discipline, but it is also central to the business strategy. We refer to this group as the agenda setters because with this level of maturity in their thought leadership program, these organizations are often defining the conversation across industries and sectors. Such is the power of their thought leadership.

We have learned about several real-world examples on the potential impact thought leadership had on those companies in the last few chapters. The next chapter encapsulates a list of tools that I use and recommend for kick starting your thought leadership content marketing strategy. This will be followed by interviews with companies committed to investing in thought leadership as a long-term strategy.

Leveraging Tools for Content and Thought Leadership Marketing

8 Useful Content Marketing Tools

Devising a content marketing strategy can feel overwhelming, especially if you are a newcomer. There are many free tools online that may contribute to making your content marketing campaign a little less arduous. I've listed eight of my go-to content marketing tools below.

1. **Idea Generation** (HubSpot's Blog Topic Generator)

   My team and I rely heavily on understanding our target audience and addressing their questions, pain points, objections, and so on. Every piece of content begins with an idea. Having an effective ideation tool in your arsenal will aid you in getting out of a rut when you are looking for inspiration. HubSpot's blog topic generator fulfils this need. You can just type in three nouns related to the topic you are considering, and the tool generates five ideas you can use for your blog posts.

2. **Content Creation** (Knowledge Management Templates)

   The content creation process isn't just about editorial competence. A large part of the creation process weighs in on insights from subject matter experts in your organization. I can tell you from experience that subject matter experts are often very busy people and many of them aren't masters at storytelling. This is where knowledge management templates come in handy. This tool makes it easy to store and organize expert insights from SMEs all in one place so your marketing team can use them to streamline the content creation process.

3. **Outlining** (MindMup)

   Once your team has reached a consensus on a topic, it is important to have a roadmap laid out. This map should highlight where your article is heading even before you start writing. Otherwise you could end up with a rambling mess of interesting, but disconnected, ideas. MindMup's brainstorming tool allows you to create a visually descriptive mind map of your thoughts using text bubbles, links, and images so you (and your audience) never feel the stress of disorganized thoughts.

4.   **Collaboration** (Asana)

Do you have multiple thought leaders working together on content? Asana could be your hub for teams to collaborate on content. Asana is a flexible web / mobile application that makes workflow management and communication seamless. With features such as project templates, team pages, and visually engaging dashboards, Asana makes it easier to nix the chaos of team projects. The baseline version is free for up to 15 team members.

5.   **Writing Magnetic Headlines** (CoSchedule's Headline Analyzer)

Once you have put the miles into creating a high-quality piece of content, you need to make sure the headline is just as effective. An analysis of more than four million pieces of content in "The State of Digital Media" offers insight into what makes a good headline. Make sure you are consistently creating those effective headlines with CoSchedule's headline analyzer. This tool scores headlines based on overall word balance, length, sentiment, and keywords, Furthermore, it provides a Google search preview and email subject line preview, so you know exactly how your content appears to readers.

6.   **Social Media Management** (Buffer)

Content distribution is key to maximizing the reach and impact of your efforts. With a social distribution plan in place, tools like Buffer's social media scheduler can help you manage all your social media accounts on one platform. Whether you're posting to LinkedIn, Facebook, Twitter, or Instagram, you can queue all your posts ahead of time.

7.   **Visual Content Development** (Canva)

Canva is a design tool for creating social media banners, presentations, email newsletters, and more. Canva has a free and a paid version. The paid version includes access to extra features as well as the perk of downloading your files with a transparent background. The wide range of presets and design templates can help you create bespoke images for your blog posts, so they feel and look unique.

8. **Content Performance Analysis** (BuzzSumo)

BuzzSumo is a tool that allows you to analyze which content performs the best for any given search topic and finds influencers who are likely to share that content too.

Content marketing takes a lot of effort, energy, and resources to perform well. With the help of these tools, you can execute a solid plan to engage audiences and build influence – all without digging too deep into your budget.

PART III

REAL LIFE STORIES OF THOUGHT LEADERSHIP MARKETING

IBM Global CXO Study

DIGITAL DISRUPTION: A C-SUITE STUDY BY IBM

The IBM Global CXO Study is an extensive study undertaken by IBM in conversation with over 12,000 C-suite executives. It was aimed at driving new strategies to aid business leaders to digitally reinvent themselves and outperform their competitors. This study focuses on enhancing an organization's reputation and maximizing its thought leadership output. The study comprises inputs taken from six C-suite roles spread across 112 countries and is a comprehensive approach that builds client relationships and accelerates revenue growth through thought leadership.

Source: IBM (IBM's Institute for Business Value)

Chief Executive Officer 2,148	Chief Information Officer 2,258
Chief Financial Officer 2,102	Chief Marketing Officer 2,091
Chief Human Resources Officer 2,139	Chief Operations Officer 2,116

Source: IBM (IBM's Institute for Business Value)

The challenge posed to B2B marketers today is to usher in a massive digital overhaul by investing in technology to create continuous transformation that evolves over time. Digital disruption is on the rise. The majority of the disruption is coming in from industry incumbents. In other words, according to IBM, these business leaders are leveraging their expertise to nurture talent that encompasses digital skills and platform-based business models.

72%   *C-suite executives believe that innovative industry incumbents lead the disruption in their industry*

IBV uses a very detailed approach for their research on industries, business, and functions; and they have received several great reviews for their content quality. IBM had been interviewing C-suite executives for the past 14 years – a fundamental question that was posed to them was about which external factors would impact them the most in the next 2-3 years. Changing B2B buyer preferences and higher competition in the marketplace were at the helm while technology followed. The skill sets evolved as well. The folks at IBV applied cluster analysis to demarcate segments of organizations among the 12,000 plus participants of the study. They labeled these segments as:

1. The Reinventors
2. The Practitioners
3. The Aspirationals

According to IBV, these segments/ archetypes are at different stages of digital reinvention and are looking for opportunities ahead from the vantage point.

The *'reinventors'* form 27% of the total. These are individuals that outperformed their peers in revenue growth and profitability, and further drove innovation. With a well-aligned business, they are confident of adapting to continual change. They have redirected their resources to increase their network of partners, encouraged experimentation and upskilling, and leverage data to create a great customer experience.

The *'practitioners'* – a further 37% of the total. This cohort hasn't cultivated the ability to fully match their ambitions yet. But they are ambitious, and they plan on launching new business models and are looking for ways to disrupt the industry. These individuals are ready to up the ante by considering one of the most radical business models – the platform business model.

The *'aspirationals'* seize new opportunities to move forward in the digital journey. They make up the last 36% and the biggest challenge for organizations with these individuals is to nail the vision, strategy, and resources.

The cluster analysis done by IBM is as shown here. The variables used by them to drive the analysis included:

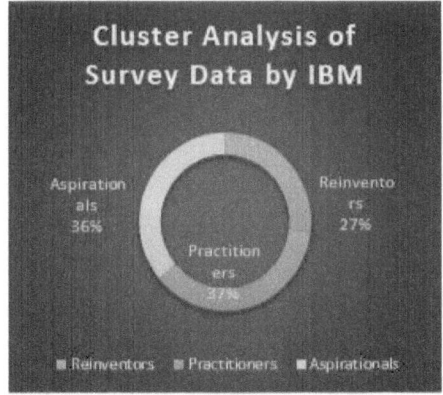

- Disrupt a new market or industry by changing the rules of the game
- Digital technologies deployed to transform interactions with customers
- Data and analytic insights used to inform business strategy
- Rapid prototyping to test and refine business strategy
- IT strategy closely aligned to business strategy
- Insights from data analysis used to constantly innovate products and services
- Short feedback and adaptation cycles to accelerate project execution

Source: IBM Global C-suite Study

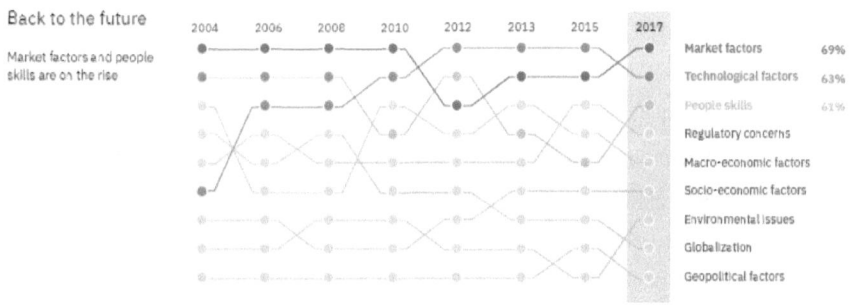

Source: IBM Global C-suite Study

The IBM study covers four key topics that hold the most relevance today,

83

Disruption (Rita Gunther McGrath (Columbia Business School), Philip Dalzell-Payne (IBM Services))

According to IBM's study, as we already mentioned above, 72% of the CXO executives interviewed stated that innovative industry incumbents spearheaded the disruption in their respective industries. The vast overhaul of digital platforms has already disrupted most industries. These incumbents have refined their digital skillset and are innovators. With the volatile nature of disruption today, C-suite executives who outperform their peers and drive innovation (the reinventors) have adapted to this ecosystem and are partnering with organizations in sharing physical assets as well as skills. Skilled incumbents have a competitive edge – their companies perform well in the long-term scheme of things and are continuously reallocating resources and personnel to explore new territory in the marketplace. These incumbents outride disruption. They have a strong understanding of the future roadmap for their industries. They rely on constant reinvention repeatedly rather than wait for a hungry competitor to overthrow them.

"Our challenge is creating vast digital change on a short timescale, disrupting our sector without disrupting our current high service levels to our customers. We are investing in technology to become more agile and enable something closer to a state of continuous transformation."

CMO, Energy and Utilities, U.K

Trust – The Path to Personalization (Joerg Niessing (INSEAD), Robert Schwartz (IBM))

86% of organizations say that they've been somewhat successful at creating experiences that cater to individual customers. 53% believe that they have been very effective at personalization. The shaping of a successful personalized customer experience is very challenging because it requires an in-depth understanding of customers i.e. humanizing them – their motivations, temperament, and quickly-shifting perceptions. A previous IBM study (The Experience Revolution) revealed some discrepancies between what C-suite executives deem is important to customers and what the customers actually perceive as valuable. In other words, there was a gap between what motivates customers and what executives understand. Analysis of C-suite executive responses to IBM's questions revealed that one key factor distinguishes the leaders (i.e. the reinventors) from other organizations. And that is the capacity to leverage data to fulfil customer needs.

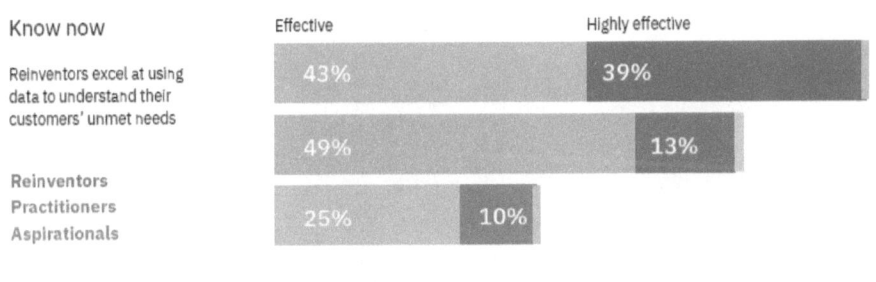

Q: How effective is your enterprise at using data to identify undefined and unmet customer needs?

Source: IBM Global C-suite Study

IBM concluded from this that many of the organizations reporting satisfaction in their customer personalization efforts were falling short of understanding their customer needs first. This could ultimately lead to higher churn rates.

Why do the reinventors succeed more than their peers at personalization?

They don't just mine a lot of data, they are design thinkers too. They empathize with their customers and study their landscape thoroughly. They have a tight knit network of close customers from whom they garner direct feedback to understand and improve the customer experience. They incorporate customer feedback into their planning process and rely on artificial intelligence and other cognitive solutions to improve the customer experience. Human motivation and behavior – are the touch points on which A.I. and cognitive solutions should focus on since they are free of unconscious bias and will reveal patterns that may otherwise remain in the dark.

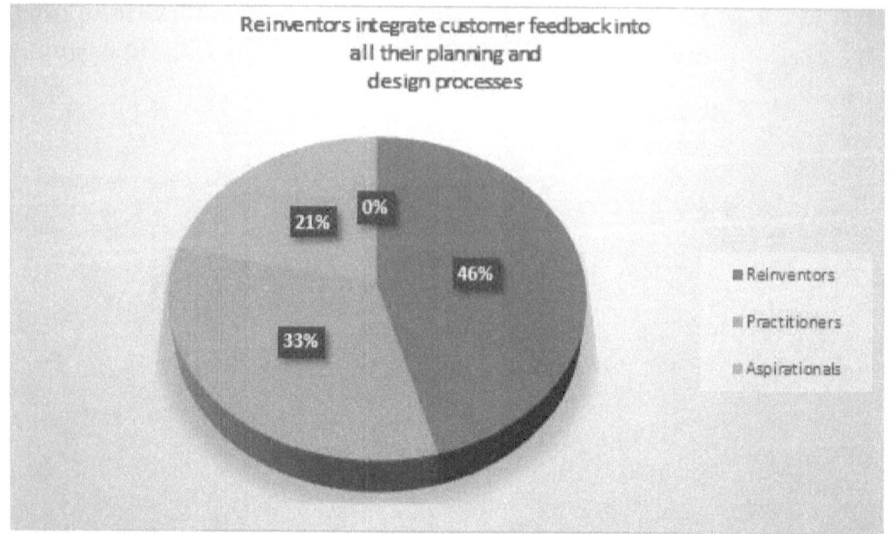

Source: IBM Global C-suite Study

Reinventors have mastered the groundwork – they study their customers closely. They don't just work towards garnering loyalty but earn and provide quantifiable reasons for customers to trust them.

What the Future Holds – Enterprise Agility with Platform Business Models (Yoram (Jerry) Wind (The Wharton School), Shanker Ramamurthy (IBM))

Collaboration leads to innovation. Executives with a strong vision are always looking for ways to experiment and empower their enterprises. The reinventors lead from a position of trust: 75% are actively soliciting ideas from their employees to develop new approaches, compared to 54% of practitioners and 38% of aspirationals. Seven in ten reinventors empower their teams to decide the best course of action.

Innovation (Amy C. Edmondson (Harvard Business School), Christine Wyatt (IBM))

Thought leaders with a strong vision always anticipate change.

These leaders position their organizations for the future and encourage employees to move beyond just workforce cogs and become problem solvers. Collaboration will surely pave the path for innovation. With employee upskilling and talent development at the fore, leadership

times are revamping their organizational structures to optimize business processes that support the vision of the company in the long term. Senior leadership promote continual dialogue and transparency with their employees to develop and nurture fresh initiatives that empower employees and their teams to take the ideal course of action. In this IBM study, C-suite executives have clearly stated that investing in talent and developing the skills of management are at the top of the list. Key areas of improvement would be:

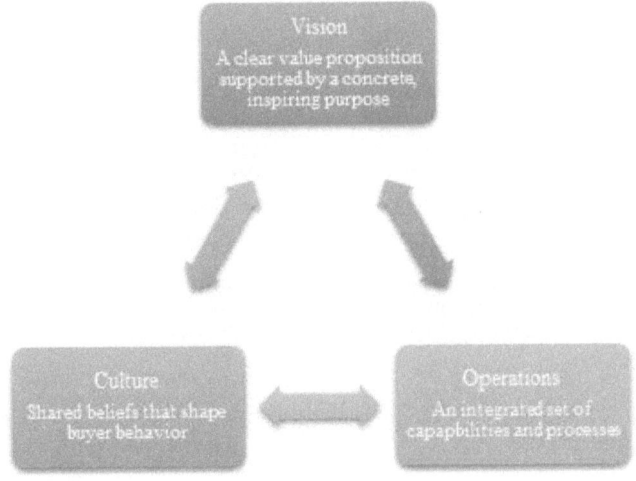

The Leaders Triangle

Source: IBM Global C-suite Study

- Dynamic Vision – ensuring that employees understand the objectives and long-term vision of the company
- Open Dialogue – where leadership teams actively seek out inputs from their employees to develop new ideas
- Agile Operations – drive the adoption of the required skill set and resources and invest in continuous employee development

The IBM global CXO study entailed asking a specific set of questions to obtain executives' strategic mindset and their commitments to digitally reinvent their enterprises. The entire report can be found on IBM's IBV webpage.

Trelleborg Marine Systems

If you can't beat them, change the rules of the game.

This example shows how Stein IAS (a globally-renowned marketing agency) achieved a 10% email click through rate and 15 editorial hits for Trelleborg Marine Systems that resulted in Stein IAS getting nominated for a B2B marketing award as a result.

Trelleborg Marine Systems is an engineering company with over 40 years of experience in designing, manufacturing, and installing protective equipment for many of the world's large commercial seaports. One of the company's key product lines is marine fenders made from high-quality industrial grade rubber, which provides the first line of defense between a berthing vessel and port infrastructure.

The Objective

In addition to lobbying PIANC, the industry body was responsible for marine product guidelines to mandate third-party testing on all fender systems. The key performance indicators included:

- Email: click-through rates of 10% across all campaigns
- PR: 15 editorial hits (at least 50% of them were in tier-1 media platforms)
- Social Media: 100 referral visits to the campaign landing page

The Campaign Timescale: June 2015–April 2016

Background

Trelleborg had been facing stiff competition from copycat competitors. Many potential ill-informed customers were preparing to take a risk on low cost and cheaper alternatives. Speaking on high quality expertise for port safety and maintenance was not changing buyer behavior for a portion of the market significant enough to pose a threat to the future of Trelleborg fenders. Although Trelleborg was attracting attention to the importance of rubber quality, the guidelines of PIANC remained unchanged and it left the door unattended to the influx of inferior products that were eating away at Trelleborg's market share. Stein IAS and Trelleborg collaborated to shift focus from product quality promotion to industry quality promotion with the goal of changing the PIANC guidelines on fender specifications to include third-party testing on rubber compound quality.

The Target Audience

The ultimate target was PIANC – the industry body responsible for marine product guidelines. But to build momentum towards a change in the guidelines that included third-party testing of rubber compounds in fenders, a key part of the strategy was to build the 'industry quality' conversation among the key decision makers and influencers in port construction and maintenance.

How Did They Do It?

Distributed via email, online advertising, PR, and social, the key thought leadership assets were:

The Barometer Report:

Back in 2010, Trelleborg launched an industry-wide annual survey, gathering in-depth insights from the market on port and terminal infrastructure and industry issues. What followed was the launch of the barometer report, a key content piece intended to establish Trelleborg as a thought leader on industry growth, changes in regulations and regional trends. The first edition revealed that the majority of those responsible for procurement of berthing and docking products were solely concerned with price. As a result, port owners, operators, and contractors were settling for lower standards and compromising long-term performance. The barometer report gave Trelleborg data and insights on current thinking while highlighting the gap in safety concerns which were high and the quality of fenders which was overall substandard.

In 2015, Trelleborg published the Barometer Report, in a new interactive, online format. Its results showed an extremely positive shift in the mindset of the market. Five years ago, nobody considered rubber compound specification, never mind implementing it. Now, almost 30% are in fact implementing it. Even more encouragingly, just over 30% also stated that they request or commission third party testing, highlighting a change in market thinking in both, specifying quality and ensuring these standards are met in practice.

The Rubber Quality Testing Program

If you want to convince the powers that be to change guidelines to include third-party testing, why not become a third-party tester to prove that it's a good idea? In 2015, Trelleborg did just that by conducting a rigorous testing program proving the importance of ingredient mixing and the manufacturing process in fender performance, by testing fenders on-site across the globe. This provided Trelleborg with the evidence to back up its message and information to fuel the content-hungry Eloqua system, a marketing automation platform that powered its fully integrated digital marketing strategy. The first phases of the campaign were built around awareness content – raising the issue through a research-led thought leadership whitepaper and webinar. Once a prospect was suitably engaged, they received the Rubber Fender Product Brochure.

Other elements of the campaign included:

- Rubber quality webinar
- Rubber fender product brochure

Face to Face

Trelleborg further strengthened their reputation for quality by delivering technical seminars on fender specification and its importance.

Outcome

As a result of Stein IAS' thought leadership, PIANC agreed to include the need for third-party testing in its guidelines and review any required procedures for fender selection too, to include more stringent materials and performance testing. Trelleborg's efforts in 2015 were rewarded with the inclusion of frequent feature articles in PIANC's e-newsletter, 'Sailing Ahead' and its yearbook.

The first phases of the campaign were built around 'awareness' content – raising the issue through a research-led leadership whitepaper and webinar.

Other results included emails promoting the Barometer Report – receiving a huge open rate of 17.2% and conversion rate of 44%. The 2015 rubber quality campaign generated:

- 700+ whitepaper downloads
- 500+ webinar views
- 34 editorial hits (65% in Tier-1 media)
- 211,974 opportunities to see
- 170+ visits referred to the campaign landing page

Grist – The Value of B2B Thought Leadership

This case study talks about a survey that was done by Grist to understand how executives use thought leadership to establish an organization as a thought leader with credibility. Independent research company Coleman Parkes collaborated with Grist to survey over 200 senior executives from FTSE 350 companies, to understand when, how, and why they reached for thought leadership material produced by their advisers. When asked about what irks them about thought leadership, three reasons stood out. Most respondents said that they disliked content that was:

- Too generic – not directly relevant to me (63%)
- Lacked original insight or ideas (58%)
- Promoted the adviser rather than addressing my problems (53%)

In other words, the best way to alienate a chosen audience is to produce generic, unoriginal content written from the supplier point of view rather than the client point of view – this is how stock content marketing is done. Just churning out content to attract customers without any real value. As we had seen in an earlier chapter, content marketing and thought leadership aren't the same, even though they sometimes work together towards a common goal. Instinctively, every marketer should know this is the wrong way to do things yet those in receipt of thought leadership are obviously experiencing it every day.

To underscore these areas of the failure, the survey asked respondents what qualities they found most valuable in thought leadership. The top three responses were:

- Fresh thinking: exploring issues or challenges from new and different perspectives (46%)
- Forward-thinking: analyzing important or emerging trends (32%)
- Evidence-led: containing robust data (29%)

Original and specific, in other words.

Finally, it's worth considering the other reasons why senior executives are turned off by thought leadership. Namely, material that was:

- Too conceptual – without recommendations (47%)
- Featured unsubstantiated opinions (40%)
- Difficult/boring to read (38%)

These responses were chosen in fewer numbers, but they were pertinent, nonetheless. Treat all six responses – and the top three in particular – as a checklist. Test every piece of thought leadership commissioned and written against the list. If it fails the test by being on the list, then don't bother publishing it.

More Success Stories in Thought Leadership Marketing

Wipro

Wipro – a current leading provider of IT services and consulting entered the technology business in 1981. They have since expanded to digital transformation for global enterprises as well. With a history of investing in domain-specific technology and thought leadership, they set up a focused research council to drive their thought leadership agenda. This council worked closely with Ivy League schools such as Harvard, Stanford, Wharton, LBS, and UCLA, among others. The council devised forward thinking research reports in collaboration with academia which helped shape the thinking of their prospects as well as showcase Wipro's expertise in cutting-edge technologies. This further helped build a solid relationship with these influencers that improved their overall brand audit score on thought leadership by 25 basis points.

Knowledge@Wharton

Wharton's thought leadership program covers many different disciplines and is available to marketers in the form of academic research, books, and more. Knowledge@Wharton offers organizations the opportunity to highlight their thought leadership expertise and gain credibility through co-branding initiatives. Knowledge@Wharton created a platform to foster innovation called the Innovation Tournament. This platform was developed with a similar model to the hit show American Idol, i.e. first a future-looking problem statement was delineated. Academic professionals across the globe were then invited to showcase their solutions to a high-profile jury panel that evaluated the ideas and selected finalists. These finalists were assigned mentors from the industry who helped them fine tune their ideas further. The finalists presented these ideas to the jury and the winners were awarded a cash prize as well as facility access and mentorship to transform their ideas into reality – an interesting thought leadership marketing approach to showcase how innovation and expertise could be demonstrated while engaging the key target audience.

Cisco

Future of Workforce – an initiative undertaken by Cisco where they partnered with experts and thought leaders to pinpoint drivers that could potentially change the future of workforce on a global scale. The initiative included research, case studies, roundtable discussions, webinars, an online community to develop potential working models and processes, and a book as well. These actions collectively showcased Cisco as a thought leader in this space. Workforce 2020, according to Cisco, is a globalized, virtualized cohort of workers whose identity is being shaped by the generational, technical, economic, and social market transitions that are taking place everywhere. Another trend that's running in unison with globalization is the changing demographics. The average age of a knowledge worker today has reduced drastically – the next gen employees are smart, ambitious, and tech savvy, which also make them agile and more responsive than their predecessors. Futurists predict that by 2020, building employee value will transgress from an organizational expectation to an economic necessity.

Hot Spot Movement

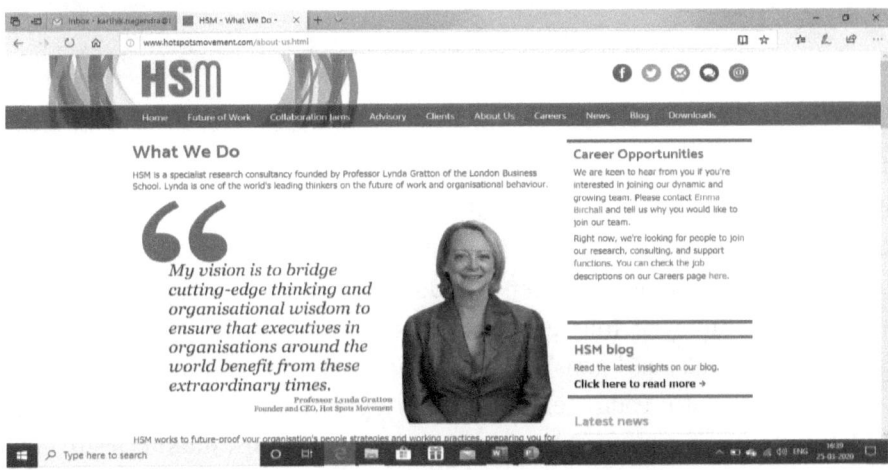

HSM is a specialist research consultancy founded by Professor Lynda Gratton of the London Business School. Lynda is one of the world's leading thinkers on the future of work and organizational behavior. HSM works to future-proof your organization's people strategies and working practices, preparing organizations for the future of work. Drawing on cutting-edge insights from academia, they help companies attract and engage with tomorrow's talent, to foster innovation and enhance performance. Whether organizations want to harness the collective wisdom of your employees, future-proof their organization, or ensure their Inclusion and Diversity strategy is fit for purpose, they offer a variety of solutions to suit companies' needs through jams - their online platform and bespoke research and advisory.

Ricoh – An Agent of Change for Technology Transformation

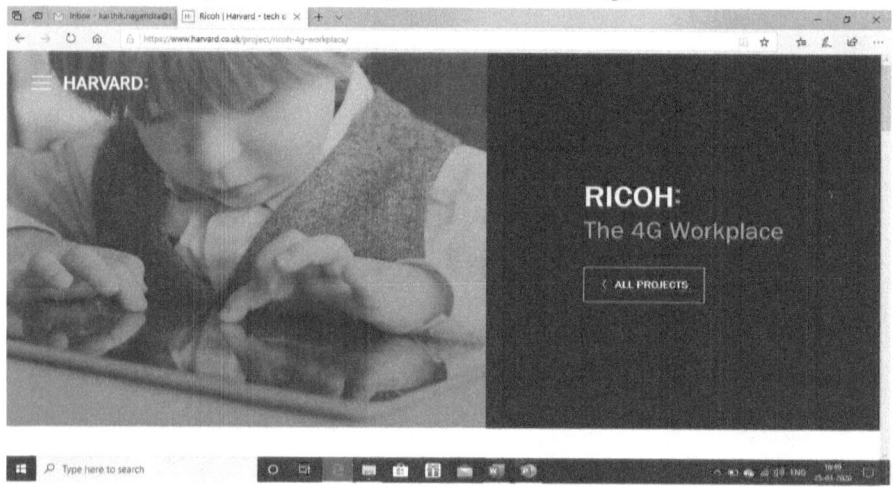

Ricoh is a Japanese multinational electronics company. Ricoh was successful in grabbing the attention of C-suite executives by focusing its thought leadership strategy on a niche challenge faced by multi-generational workplaces spanning different industries and geographies. These workplaces employed four generations, often comprising baby boomers, gen X, millennials, and gen Y. These people are now coming together for collaboration with each generation having a different affiliation with technology. Ricoh ran several senior executive workshops and surveyed 3500 workers from 22 countries to gain insights for their 4G workplace report. This report highlighted key trends and issues and was backed with social content, infographics, and press releases. The campaign had an outreach of 65 million people in Europe and comprised more than 850 pieces of media coverage, over 200,000 impressions on social media, and 6000 unique visits on its landing page. The key success factor here was Ricoh's masterstroke in taking a widely relevant issue and bringing in a unique perspective on it that appeals to the media.

Source (b2bmarketing.net)

Oracle – Providing a Personalized Roadmap for Brands

Oracle Financial Services demonstrated its understanding of changing customer expectations by leveraging three strategic partnerships that targeted prospects through digital and direct channels. Oracle ran a campaign that included teaser videos of a panel of 16 to 21-year-olds sharing their views on banking and finance – this led into a microsite with an event titled 'Meet the Disruptors'. The event garnered a lot of attention and brought together senior banking executives face-to-face with next generation financial consumers. Post the event, attendees were able to download a report and soundbite videos. Multiple email campaigns and social media brought various elements together.

"The live event, being completely unscripted, wasn't without risk. But that's what made both the event and the content it generated even more compelling. It has demonstrated that significant reward can come from calculated risk"

– Rachel Fraser (Marketing Director, Oracle Financial Services)

By providing a personalized roadmap to encourage digital transformation among brands, Oracle positioned itself as an innovative thought leader. The peer panel and event created quite the buzz and was attended by 52 senior executives. Data was captured from 626 senior banking executives who downloaded the report. Furthermore, the videos received more than 32000 unique visits.

Source (b2bmarketing.net)

BlackRock

Asset manager BlackRock's iShares division took a topic that has a negative perception in the industry – 'volatility' and presented it as an opportunity, through a two-part campaign targeting wealth managers. The first part, 'Foundation' messaging was based on predictive, quarterly market themes that focused on a particular asset class iShares believed would be very impactful in the coming quarter. The second part, 'Flare' messages were quick fire advertising based on market changes that could trigger portfolio changes. Together, these helped iShares to become a trusted source of information. The ongoing 'Foundation' messages helped build trust, while speedy delivery of the 'Flare' messages gives wealth managers an audience that demands constant updates to make smarter investment decisions for clients – this was the reliability that was needed. Weekly sentiment from 120 wealth managers added more clout to the campaign, as the target audience gained direct insight from its peers.

"The marketing effort around quarterly market themes has not only enabled iShares to continue to differentiate its brand using its unique investment strategy capabilities, but it has helped the iShares business capture vital flows and revenue in volatile markets"

Source (b2bmarketing.net)

Kathryn Shiplee (Head of Brand and Advertising, EMEA, BlackRock)

Arco

Safety supplier Arco built its profile as an industry leader by changing the perception of safety as a commodity. A strategic partnership with the British Safety Industry Federation (BSIF), UK's leading safety trade body, positioned Arco as a trusted expert and proactive agent of change, and added weight to its campaign. Arco stopped focusing on product promotion and delivered content that addressed industry issues, such as elevating the standard of safety equipment. By doing this, they built a relationship with their target audience first and then demonstrated how it was positioned to help. By educating brands with failing products, Arco achieved industry-level impact. The company further received excellent brand perception scores and was awarded Superbrand status in 2016.

Source (b2bmarketing.net)

Experts Speak

Understanding your niche as a thought leader – not an easy undertaking by any means. If you can learn where your expertise has the most value with customers, you will eventually start to pick up clues on what works and dive into the nitty gritty of thought leadership content to engage them. But being an expert is just half the job. Your expertise is probably valued by some, but at the end of the day, it will be your personality and prowess combined that ultimately draws people to your message. Thought leadership messaging should showcase content with your personal voice and advocacy – this makes you stand out in a crowd. Your audience will spot unscrupulous jargon from a mile away so don't engage in any kind of unnecessary self-promotion. This is a progressive journey that requires years of dedication, charisma, talent, and skills. Many companies with complex B2B business models and sales cycles are slowly ramping up their content and thought leadership strategies to build authenticity.

Here's a look at some interviews I did on how a few companies have remained committed to the ideal of guidance and leadership by investing in thought leadership marketing to entice prospects.

Sunder Madakshira, Head of Marketing, Adobe India

Sunder at Adobe stated that marketing is moving towards sales and content-based sales. Marketing needs to have the ability to convince customers since the confidence level is different for buyers and sellers – building trust helps in this aspect since it speaks to the authenticity of the brand. According to Sunder, it is an under communicated world. Mere clicks on websites isn't good customer engagement. Excess content and channels don't always work. The main goal of thought leadership marketing should be to increase revenue for the organization as well as test marketing programs.

He has a steadfast view on marketing efforts. Marketers nowadays waste time talking about efforts. The CMO builds goals by aligning marketing goals to the company goals – the important part is to get the CEO to listen. They have a CMO and CIO community class as part of a thought leadership program. Here, they conduct educational workshops for buyers. He predicts the B2B marketing scenario to be better integrated with artificial intelligence and machine learning. The B2B marketing landscape will be more consultative and will slow down as a result of these consultants coming to the fore.

Raghunandan Rao – Global Head of Marketing, Bosch

Bosch has been working on technologies like A.I. and blockchain. They believe the application of thought leadership will primarily be for lead generation. The B2B landscape is shifting. We are moving towards an age of technology-driven marketing. Buyers do their homework. There is more information symmetry today. Involving your customers in future technology will go a long way to improve thought leadership. In the B2B buying space, personalization is getting more important. Bosch has been working with SPAR on personalization. By campaigning together, they wanted to project themselves as a technologically driven consumer experience company.

Purnima Menon, Chief Marketing Officer, Marlabs

Purnima works with Marlabs – a company committed to enabling digital solutions for their clients and partners around the world. They are centered in New Jersey with 2,300 employees across offices in US, Canada, Germany, and India. Poornima states that the ability to be consultative and partnering with clients to demonstrate thought leadership marketing at the initial stage of the buying process is very important. With the evolution of the B2B landscape, digital has evolved over the last ten years. Buyers now have multiple options to choose from and consume knowledge at a rapid pace. Impended relationships may not work anymore. Furthermore, collaborative thought leadership content consistently provides real, tangible solutions.

Promit Sanyal, Chief Marketing Officer, Moonraft Innovation Labs

Promit helps accelerate marketing processes to create value for organizations. He believes the consumer is changing at a rapid pace. B2B sales is lagging because of the focus shift from sales to marketing (digital and modern). Most customers are already equipped with enough information. He further states that the primary challenge now is, firms are at a stage where thought leadership marketing aids a contributive role in some capacity, but most organizations don't have enough resources to invest in thought leadership marketing. His goal is to focus on the U.S market in order to increase the market share. He has just started with account-based marketing and is trying to figure out what to do with content. Promit believes the best thought leadership content is client testimonials via video once a project is completed.

Anubhav Arora, Head – Strategic Marketing, Indegene

Indegene serves as a digital transformation partner for leading life sciences companies globally. In a post pandemic world, we will see a blend of physical and digital models. Digital's prominence has been the priority over the last few months. When Indegene works with these companies, we try to figure out the right blended experience for our customers. Externally, pharma and healthcare overall is accelerating digital evolution. They are happy to work with partners like us. At this point, cutting through the noise is important. We have built a strong base around thought leadership and how we can handhold companies through the entire journey and work with them in different aspects. The question on most industry leaders' minds is whether they are up to date on the happenings in the industry, what their peers are doubling down on, what new ideas can accelerate digital capabilities. We leveraged thought leadership like research, digital council, among others, to emerge as strategic thinkers. The industry, in the light of this uncertainty, is looking for partners who can talk at a thought leadership level.

Vimal Abraham- Former Governing Council Member, NASSCOM Marketing Forum

Nasscom's thought leadership marketing forum saw B2B, B2C, and tech-based marketers come together. They believed in peer-to-peer learning irrespective of the company size. The lines between B2B and B2C are getting blurred. This is a change that has been in effect for some time now. Buyers have become more aware. The decision-making psychology between B2B and B2C is similar with the risk being higher in the B2B space. Establishing an emotional connect is important for brand messaging. Thought leadership is about solving problems without the intent of selling a solution to a customer – a spray and pray approach would be impractical. Furthermore, thought leadership marketing is a long-term solution. Thought leadership and content marketing should work collectively. Also, the price point should be low and attractive enough to ensure repeat customers. You'd need to convince your business leaders that linear growth is the way forward.

Rafiq Dossani- Director, RAND Center for Asia Pacific Policy, and Professor, Pardee RAND Graduate School

B2B consumers are evolving. They are becoming increasingly aware of areas where they know they can benefit. The first area is artificial intelligence and big data. For e.g., for marketing in the manufacturing space, the role of A.I. is shaping the manufacturing process and addressing consumer needs is becoming increasingly important. The second is that B2B consumers understand that their marketing is being consumed both in the B2B and B2C space by patrons who are aware of the latest trends. So, finding unique marketing insights becomes ever more important. Third, there is less of 'commoditization' in decision making and greater expectations of 'bespoke approaches' – this requires better, more sophisticated marketing. Furthermore, B2B customers are becoming more like B2C customers. These B2C customers have always demanded bespoke capabilities and now B2B customers are demanding it as well. This is where thought leadership plays a crucial role in helping B2B brands embrace brand advocacy. The advantage of generating good ideas and delivering unique insights has never been greater due to the increased collaborativeness of this new paradigm. Take Microsoft's recent move to the cloud – a successful execution of a thought leadership marketing campaign. Microsoft's move to the cloud despite being a late entrant along with the marketing campaign that supported it was very effective. Technology will play a crucial role in thought leadership marketing. It will be to ensure greater collaborativeness and create more sophisticated campaigns based on A.I. / big data.

PART IV

TRENDS IN THOUGHT LEADERSHIP MARKETING. WHAT DOES THE FUTURE HOLD?

Benefits of Thought Leadership Marketing

The preceding sections gave us some useful insights into what thought leadership encompasses. We studied the 5F Model, ITSMA model and learned that as thought leadership marketers, we need to heavily focus on adding a personal touch when engaging with our target audience. Our focus on content-related initiatives needs to be perfectly aligned with buyers' needs and demographics. The key takeaway from the ITSMA study was that we need to raise the bar when we engage with these buyers, on their terms, not ours. Thought leadership is emerging as a powerful way for brands to assert their dominance, boost brand awareness, and increase their market share.

"Thought leadership content should be informative and embody innovative and actionable components that, in time, because of their effectiveness and contributions, can become accepted industry practices. There are many worthwhile approaches of generating high-quality content. What's essential is to be extremely attentive to the needs and wants of the audience for the material."

– Bruce Rogers, Chief Insights Officer, Forbes

Elevating the profile of thought leaders around what the brand wants to be known for has a direct benefit in many different areas.

Better Publicity, More Brand Value

Being an established thought leader opens doors to more PR opportunities. If you are an influential expert on a topic, you have a better chance of landing interviews. Reporters will want to talk to you and write about what you have on offer. Your customers will start to deem you as an authority figure who understands the business needs of the industry. This will eventually lead to more sales and hopefully, better profit margins.

Higher Credibility and Trust

When you and your brand provide accurate innovation on a consistent basis, your customers are more likely to find you trustworthy; you further garner more respect and make it likely for customers to choose your business over a competitor's.

More Charitability = More Loyalty

When you assist and support your customers with demonstrated hands-on expertise, you make your customers happy. Giving away freebies in the form of blog posts, videos, product demos, etc. will empower the people in your niche. The added value will build loyalty and increase market share. By building a consistent repository of valuable information, you engage closely with potential clients that may turn them into paying customers down the road.

Optimized Marketing Budgets

Once you have doubled down on your thought leadership strategy, you can cut back on your traditional marketing spends. Why? Thought leadership is often cost-effective. It can reach a much wider audience with a positive word-of-mouth.

Better Business Opportunities

Thought leadership can often open doors to new ventures and business opportunities that previously would have seemed implausible. When more people connect with your brand messaging, it improves your brand value and recognition – which could pave the way to expanding your brand footprint in other countries.

Increased Sales and Lifetime ROI

A good brand reputation established through good thought leadership can improve your sales funnel. The credibility you have gained through your efforts will improve your lead generation and attract more potential customers in the long run. This will also encourage repeat purchases and give you a better ROI.

Comprehensive Omni-channel Approach

When you develop thought leadership content for multiple channels, you give customers the freedom of gleaning your content and insights via their preferred platform. Those who like reading short articles can benefit from blogs, those who prefer audio can listen in to a podcast, and others who lean more towards videos can benefit from webinars, product demos, and conference videos.

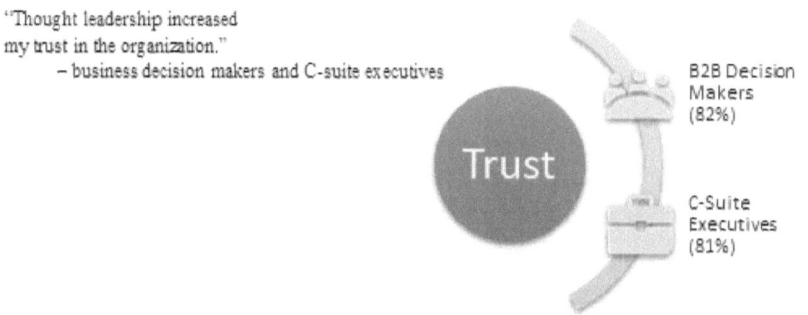

(Michael Brenner, Marketing Insider Group, 2019)

San Francisco based EdTech firm Degreed is an LMS platform with over four million people across 250+ organizations, focused on enabling and recognizing skill sets for professionals. They provide lifelong learning by tracking and optimizing learning activities for companies and their employees to help them improve how training and learning should be done. Degreed is a thought leader in the EdTech space. One of the biggest benefits provided by Degreed is that they have established a very powerful reputation by creating exemplary whitepapers such as: How the Workforce Learns in 2016. This report is a great example of how thought leadership content has shaped Degreed into the go-to authority for anyone looking to understand the EdTech landscape today. They also produce ungated, data-driven publications that speak volumes on their innovative approach to leveraging learning management systems that encapsulates their thought leadership activities.

Another industry leader that helps companies reap the benefits of thought leadership by helping them grow their business is Sondhelm Partners. Sondhelm is a premium purveyor of brand positioning, marketing, public relations, and many other solutions for the asset management industry. They help organizations enhance their brand messaging, empower sales teams for better distribution, aid in public relations efforts to get the necessary traction and news coverage, and much more. With more than 100 years of collective experience, Sondhelm Partners, spearheaded by CEO Dan Sondhelm and a team of growth strategy experts are all dedicated to helping asset managers grow and retain a greater share of assets.

Embrace authenticity. An authentic and credible brand message armed with the capability to show their human side to customers what they truly stand for will build a genuine, long-term relationship with customers.

Challenges of Thought Leadership Marketing

Thought leadership marketing helps improve the business decision making process for anyone looking to align their problems with an industry leader through thought leadership content. However, like any other business challenge, thought leadership marketing too has its own fair share of challenges and hurdles to overcome. Wikipedia critiques the phrase 'thought leader' as an annoying example of business jargon and cynics further refer to thought leadership as 'meaningless management speak' even if the larger majority extol it as a revolutionary way forward for brands and businesses.

"Thought leaders do not become thought leaders by trying to be one; that's an external focus that only satisfies the ego and blocks true enlightenment on any subject. A thought leader has a singular, internal focus on achieving mastery of a particular discipline."

– Sam Fiorella

With so much noise in the marketplace about thought leadership, brands do often find it difficult to stay afloat even if they have a viable offer on the table for their customers. There are often multiple challenges that lower the potential of thought leadership strategies. Let's look at a few of them.

Overabundance of Content

Creating content is a good thing – when it has a specific theme and purpose. But how much content is too much content? Many thought leaders create content that holds relevance in some capacity. However, if there isn't a central purpose to creating it or if there isn't a direct link between the content and the customer's problem statement, the brand message gets watered down to a trickle and is probably lost forever in the multitude of unwanted blogs and articles. Secondly, once you create content, you need to find ways to monetize it. The content creation process is the primary goal but the inability to market it effectively to extend reach and impact prospective customers will just render the entire operation moot. You need to strike a balance. Between impactful content creation and monetization, you should look at metrics that can quantify your efforts in order to measure your success.

Copious Amounts of Misinformation

Every day, a lot of information is pumped out – via the internet, media, and so on. A lot of times, most of the information we see is just XYZ asking you to blindly follow them purely on faith on the premise of 'value' – delusions of grandeur! About 55-60% of information just causes a great deal of confusion among customers. Which makes it even more difficult for a trusted source to gain some headway into enticing customers.

ACCORDING TO A STUDY, 35% OF B2B BUYERS SPEND 1–3 HOURS PER WEEK REVIEWING THOUGHT LEADERSHIP CONTENT AND ABOUT 50% OF B2B MARKETERS BELIEVE CREDIBLE THOUGHT LEADERSHIP BUILDS TRUST IN THEIR ORGANIZATION. ANOTHER SURVEY STATED THAT 63% OF GLOBAL CITIZENS SAY CEOS ARE NOT AT ALL OR SOMEWHAT CREDIBLE.

The Generation Divide

Considering that majority of B2B buyers today are millennials, another point that can cause grief to thought leaders is the generation gap. Most established thought leaders today are in the 40-60 age group. Millennials are often impulsive decision makers – brand loyalty isn't ingrained into their psyche. They often jump ship at the first feel of a downside when vested with a brand. Thought leaders, especially senior thought leaders, need to understand the kind of audience they are dealing with. With a big divide in age gap and habits, it would be impractical for thought leaders and these potential buyers to agree on everything.

Scaling Up (or) Down?

When creating thought leadership content, it is important to deploy content on whatever platforms you have finalized in a timely manner. Also, you must ensure it reaches the right people in the right amount in the right medium. A webinar or a product demo, for example, can work for a small group of people. A keynote speech on the other hand may work for a slightly bigger crowd. Videos and blogs are great for online consumption to hundreds or even thousands of people. It all depends on your thought leadership strategy – scaling your leadership projects and revenues is like threading a needle. A little to the left or to the right and you have missed your mark.

Overcoming Excess Babble

Today, there are close to quarter of a million podcasts and radio stations around us. Many television channels are converting to podcasts. There are over a billion websites on the internet. News and advertisements everywhere! So, in order to overcome all this noise and be heard, as a thought leader, you need to listen to the people asking for assistance and, more importantly, you need to have a satisfactory solution to their problem. You need to build a relationship with them first, before you become a trusted source. Guide your customers in the right direction and help them help themselves.

Thought leadership within an organization has its own challenges too.

Within your own business too, there are many challenges that your very own thought leaders or SMEs could face while drawing up a thought leadership strategy. (Crade Bidings, Firebrand) made three crucial points to derive the best possible outcomes from a thought leadership strategy.

1. **Engagement** – If you haven't double checked to see if your senior leaders and executives have bought in to your thought leadership position, it may pose a problem. Lackluster engagement with your stakeholders will be problematic in the success of your campaign – both internally and externally. It will just end up being a short-lived, uninterested stunt with no senior commitment to excite your internal and external audience.

2. **Connectivity** – Interweaving the sales, marketing, finance, and human resources teams in your organization effectively is key to building meaningful connections and morale. You need to set up campaigns to aid your client-facing individuals to connect to your thought leadership content in a meaningful way so that they can then market it to the outside world.

3. **Packaging** – This includes deciding what content works best for what situation. Revisiting what has worked in the past will help you deliver tailor-made solutions to your market. Researching where your customers get their information from, how they like to consume it, whether they like interacting face-to-face, etc. are great touch points that you can siphon back to your team to package and use to good effect. Another facet to consider is sustenance. Thought leadership strategies take longer to bear fruit. But many companies expect immediate results and don't stay invested for very long. Guiding senior management and C-suite executives is key to having retrofit solutions depending on the intention of the campaign and the mission.

Whether you are trying to help a client find their sweet spot in a B2B marketing activity, or if you are trying to be a thought leader, addressing all the above challenges are essential to beat the obstacles that are likely to arise in front of you. Inculcating a culture of problem-solving and out-of-the-box thinking will determine how your brand engages with stakeholders – both internal and external. The companies that do this efficiently will go the distance in making their voices heard.

Roadmap for the Future of Thought Leadership

We are progressing through a disruptive digital era where buyers are becoming increasingly tech-savvy and well-informed. Business models need to realign with B2B buyer belief systems and perceptions since it often changes in the blink of an eye. Their increased expectations of an intricate campaign delivery system and higher ROI are convincing brands to step up their thought leadership game plan. Companies and leaders are looking to rapidly grow their businesses while also probing to thwart competitors in the same space. As corporations and brands look to leverage thought leadership to keep up with the ever-changing expectations of the B2B buyer today, the smartest marketers are agile and able to quickly adapt to change. From experimenting in A.I. and refining how we use big data, to connecting with consumers on their own terms and building brand loyalty with authentic storytelling – there are many trends that will shape the future of thought leadership.

THE BEST PREDICTOR OF FUTURE SUCCESS IS ADAPTABILITY. A PROVEN TRACK RECORD, TRADITION, AND CREDIBILITY HOLD

THE KEY TO SUCCESSFUL THOUGHT LEADERSHIP. CREDIBILITY SHOULD BE BALANCED WITH AGILITY.

Embracing changing trends means visionaries and industry experts will have a great deal of influence because clients would now be looking to these experts to embrace change and become trustful navigators in specialized fields.

Better Data Hygiene

Most marketers recognize the huge potential of big data, but they're also overwhelmed by the unprecedented volume and variety of unstructured information. Gathering data isn't enough – marketers must figure out how to separate the useful consumer insights from the larger stockpile. In our experience, with clearer data signals, marketers can use relevant insights to develop smarter, more targeted campaigns. And it's not just about the right data, but how quickly companies learn from this data to optimize the consumer experience. If you want to drive stronger daily active use of your technology product, you need to delve into what's working, what isn't, and how you can improve. This is also true for B2B marketers – how they are buying, retargeting, and using relevant data to improve the brand message, content, and the experience they are offering to customers.

Art and Science – Two Facets to Successful Content Marketing

With the proliferation of analytics tools for measuring content performance, the way marketers value content is evolving. We've already seen the interest building towards machine learning to identify behavioral patterns – next is leveraging this data to smarten creative strategy. Successful content marketing will depend heavily on a marketer's ability to quickly identify pertinent data of how consumers engage with content and how much data is relevant for informed decision making. Today, every interaction that a customer has with your content is an opportunity to build a relationship with them and ultimately bring them one step closer to making a purchase-related decision. By the same token, if the experience you are delivering isn't personalized to their needs, the chances of your efforts being perceived as 'successful' are very few. The reality is that there is no mold for marketers to mass produce thought leadership pieces, so marketers need to rethink their content and distribution by channel, keeping the broader customer experience in mind.

Foundation for Deeper A.I. Integration

Corporations are starting to take artificial intelligence and its impact seriously. Last year, a lot of chatter about A.I revolved around its huge implications and how to use it in the short term. Unfortunately, all the short-term focus has set unrealistic expectations about what's 'possible' versus what is 'still years in the making'. Marketers are already using A.I. in ad exchanges and campaign optimization. If marketers want to remain competitive, they need to explore better ways of integrating A.I. into the customer experience with chatbots and automation to supplement their customer engagement efforts, among other things.

Authentic Storytelling Improves Brand Loyalty

Smart marketers understand that modern consumers are self-directed. But consumers aren't just seeking content – they are seeking personalized experiences. In other words, they yearn for content that does more than just promote a product. The key is to start small, identify what works, and then chart out a cohesive campaign that tells an authentic story – across multiple channels, connecting with people in real-time, no matter where they are.

Digital Display Ads at a Crossroads

It is no secret that display ads aren't as effective as they used to be. 2017 was a tumultuous year in digital ad land. But despite the rise in ad-blocking software, marketers have been increasing their investments in mobile, social, and programmatic ads. The way we see it, it's time for marketers to really consider the value of display – especially on mobile. And use data insights to determine which tactics are effective in order to invest their ad dollars wisely. In line with this, we continue to see brands and marketers evolve and use a broader mix of media options, from display to native video and mobile advertising. Also, augmented and virtual reality are emerging as an impactful means to host live content across platforms quickly – this content can be personalized and tweaked for the audience. Some of the most successful brands in the world today are focused on delivering a superior customer experience. Marketers must make sure they have the right technology and customer data to allow them to deliver relevant content and experiences, across channels, at the right time. With many complex touch points and a decision journey for customers that is constantly changing, tapping into these trends is a must for marketers and brands to win big.

Increasing Complexity in Consumer Purchasing Decisions

Today, multiple media platforms from YouTube to Facebook and Instagram are being used by consumers to make shopping and business decisions – it's becoming increasingly hard to segment people that buy certain products than it used to be. Segmentation is getting more and more complex. A customer could very likely purchase one high-end product and another low-end product at the same time. They often transact with an unbalanced mix of emotions and rationale. Customers value innovation and tradition over prices. If a brand offers a solution that solves a complex business problem but costs more revenue, these consumers would be willing to go the extra mile and spend more capital with the brand.

Personalized Product Design and Communication Will Be More Prevalent

The advent of data analytics, social media, and flexible manufacturing has resulted in more companies learning to offer customized products and designs. This trend is reaching a growing number of industries, especially the healthcare sector. While pharmaceutical and healthcare companies continue to see all patients and offer treatment equally, this will eventually shift towards personalized medication based on patient demographics related to age, sex, weight, and medical history. Keep an eye out for other industries to start adopting similar practices.

Mobile Communications – Center of Marketing Engagement

There have been rumblings in the press about WhatsApp giving Facebook their users' phone numbers to deliver targeted ads. Receiving a marketing message or notification about one of your favorite products may seem a little intrusive, but then so is telemarketing. And that hasn't disappeared completely. Look out for companies that communicate with consumers on their mobile devices.

Transparency Will Dictate Brand-Customer Relationships

Businesses are realizing that they cannot escape the transparency of social media. More companies are learning the hard truth of not being transparent enough. Not just heavy fines from authorities, but also loss in loyal customers and business.

Personalized Data-driven Marketing Will Become More Friendly

Companies learn a lot about who you are and what you like by leveraging big data. And they will target and engage you in the most effective way depending on who you are and what your habits say about you. Spam cannot be eliminated yet, but companies that figure out how to stop casting their one-size-fits-all net and start targeting people in a more meaningful way can expect better results.

Emergence of Better, More Accurate Metrics

Until recently, justifying and measuring the impact of decisions had been a major challenge for marketers. Today, there are many ways to measure online activity – Facebook likes, clicks on articles, and so on. Facebook was recently caught amplifying data of how many videos were viewed on their platform. Think about the consequences for advertisers and brands who thought they were getting more bang for their buck! But this should change soon. If you didn't know how much of your advertising budget was wasted, this number should be somewhere closer to 20% soon. Budget estimation will probably never be perfect, but digital technology is improving it. Will we ever know the exact trajectory of who views an ad and then proceeds to purchase a product? I'm not so sure. But that is what marketers dream of.

Marketing Organization – From Digital Silos to Integrated Teams

Until recently, most companies would have their digital team on one side and the marketing team on the other. It can no longer work as two separate entities. Digital must be a part of everything now – both should be fully integrated with each other. Organizations don't need just a digital strategy; what they really need to know is how to plug the digital component into the complex process of how consumers make purchasing decisions. These are just some of the main trends that might continue to evolve in B2B marketing in the foreseeable future but, there will certainly be others as well.

To conclude, innovation, questioning the status quo, and adapting to disruption – B2B marketing today and in the future will require leaders that exhibit a broad array of such skills. The first and most important precept of any thought leader is the person itself – which makes it even more important to assist potential thought leaders in becoming more aware of who they are, what motivations influence their thought leadership, and understand what inhibitions they have about the current market. Every conversation and exchange is a chance for marketers to gain insight and valuable information about potential customers, focus groups, culture, and demographics. When thought leaders cultivate awareness about their audience, they often notice subtle patterns and dynamics which give them more firepower to rise above all the digital clamor and make better, data-driven decisions. Good thought leadership expands one's capacity for awareness, especially when trying to initially break in a new market with multiple unknowns – this helps them stay grounded in their values and purpose. There is a growing number of experts practicing thought leadership effectively today. Ultimately, they strengthen awareness, trounce blind spots, and solve real problems for consumers – this in turn also enhances the leader's personal development and ultimately improves the human connect.

Awareness, Influence, Vision – three tenets that
every thought leader should emulate

In order to get to the next level of whatever you are doing, you must think and act in a wildly different way than you previously have been. You cannot get to the next phase of a project without a grander mindset, more acceleration, and extra horsepower.

– Grant Cardone (Entrepreneur, Speaker and Author)

Acknowledgments

Writing a book is harder than I thought and more rewarding than I could have ever imagined. None of this would have been possible without the support of my team - Deveshree and Prashanth who helped me carry out the research and put this book together.

I'm extremely grateful to Jessie Paul for agreeing to write the foreword for this book. Surely means a lot to me! A special thanks to Purnima Menon, Rafiq Dossani, Anubhav Arora, Sunder Madakshira, Raghunandan Rao, Dave Munn, Vimal Abraham and Promit Sanyal for taking time off their busy schedules and sharing their perspectives around this topic and adding more value to my book.

To my family for supporting me in my journey as a marketing professional and always encouraging me to pursue my dreams. So thankful to have you in my life.

Finally to all the real thought leaders who have been part of me getting there: Jessie Paul, Madan Padaki, Mukul Pandya and Arun Katiyar. I am ever grateful to you for giving me all the opportunities and sharing valuable know-how in the field of thought leadership marketing.

References

(n.d.).

Amy C. Edmondson (Harvard Business School), Christine Wyatt (IBM). (n.d.). IBM. Retrieved from https://www.ibm.com/services/insights/c-suite-study

Chloe Nicholls. (2018, July 18). *The Rise of the Modern B2B Marketer.* Retrieved from Contentive: https://www.contentive.com/

Crade Bidings, Firebrand. (n.d.). Retrieved from https://firebrandtalent. com/blog/2012/07/the-3-key-challenges-of-leveraging-your-thought-leadership-internally/

Curata. (n.d.). *Content Marketing Pyramid: A Structural Overview.* Retrieved from www.curata.com

Geoffrey James. (2012, Feb 8). *6 Emotions That Make Customers Buy.* Retrieved from Inc.: https://www.inc.com/

ITSMA. (2014). *The ITSMA Thought Leadership Maturity Model* .

Joerg Niessing (INSEAD), Robert Schwartz (IBM). (n.d.). *Trust in the journey, IBM Global C-suite Study.* IBM . Retrieved from https://www.ibm. com/services/insights/c-suite-study

Joerg Niessing, Robert Schwartz. (n.d.). Retrieved from https://www.ibm. com/services/insights/c-suite-study

Julie Schwartz, Senior VP, ITSMA. (2018). *How Executive Engage: Connecting with Customers at Every Stage of the Relationship Lifecycle* .

Lori Wizdo, Forrester. (n.d.). *Digital Disruption Is The New Normal for B2B Marketing.*

Michael Brenner, Marketing Insider Group. (2019). *What Is Thought Leadership? And When Shoud You Use It?* Retrieved from https:// marketinginsidergroup.com/content-marketing/what-is-thought-leadership-and-when-you-should-use-it/

Mulder, P. (2018). *Brand Pyramid*. Retrieved from toolshero: https://www.toolshero.com/marketing/brand-pyramid/

Rita Gunther McGrath (Columbia Business School), Philip Dalzell-Payne (IBM Services). (n.d.). *Dancing with Disruption, IBM Global C-suite Study*. IBM. Retrieved from https://www.ibm.com/services/insights/c-suite-study

Rita Gunther McGrath, Philip Dalzell-Payne. (n.d.). Retrieved from https://www.ibm.com/services/insights/c-suite-study

Yoram (Jerry) Wind (The Wharton School), Shanker Ramamurthy (IBM). (n.d.). *IBM Global C-suite Study*. IBM. Retrieved from https://www.ibm.com/services/insights/c-suite-study

Yoram (Jerry) Wind, Shanker Ramamurthy. (n.d.). Retrieved from https://www.ibm.com/services/insights/c-suite-study

https://marketinginsidergroup.com/content-marketing/what-is-thought-leadership-and-when-you-should-use-it/

https://blog.kurtosys.com/evolution-b2b-marketing-infographic/

https://knowledge.insead.edu/blog/insead-blog/how-to-build-a-brand-pyramid-8491

https://www.theceomagazine.com/business/management-leadership/the-benefits-of-thought-leadership-for-companies/

https://www.marketingweek.com/2018/05/16/b2b-marketers/

https://www.fiftyfiveandfive.com/3-biggest-b2b-marketing-challenges/

https://www.thebritagency.com/inbo`und-marketing-blog/2019-brings-new-challenges-for-b2b-marketers

https://www.lyfemarketing.com/blog/b2b-marketing-trends/

https://firstpagesage.com/thought-leadership/

https://richtopia.com/effective-leadership/key-trends-in-marketing-thought-leadership-whitepaper-included

https://www.circlesstudio.com/blog/what-is-thought-leadership/

https://www.b2bmarketing.net/en-gb/resources/b2b-case-studies/awards-case-study-stein-ias-take-thought-leadership-next-level

https://www.r2integrated.com/r2insights/evolution-of-the-b2b-buyer

https://www.onlinemarketinginstitute.org/blog/2012/10/b2b-marketing-tips-for-success/

file:///C:/Users/deves/Downloads/5386-17039-1-SM.pdf

https://www.relevance.com/blog/3-brands-that-master-b2b-thought-leadership/

https://www.lyfemarketing.com/blog/digital-marketing-vs-traditional-marketing/

https://bloomgroup.com/content/history-thought-leadership-marketing-consulting-and-it-services

https://www.imd.org/research-knowledge/articles/seven-trends-that-will-affect-the-future-of-marketing/

https://www.forbes.com/sites/forbesagencycouncil/2018/04/18/five-trends-shaping-the-future-of-marketing/#776240214d36

https://www.inc.com/geoffrey-james/6-emotions-that-make-customers-buy.html https://www.quirks.com/articles/how-b2b-marketers-can-use-cognitive-biases-to-their-advantage

https://www.toolshero.com/marketing/brand-pyramid/

https://www.socialmediatoday.com/news/study-b2b-marketers-underestimate-the-power-of-thought-leadership/554499/

https://www.edelman.com/research/b2b-thought-leadership

https://www.socialmediaexaminer.com/thought-leadership-with-phil-mershon/

https://thoughtleadershipleverage.com/3-challenges-that-authors-and-thought-leaders-face/

https://digitalmarketinginstitute.com/blog/digital-selling-and-social-selling-do-you-know-the-difference

https://www.dummies.com/business/marketing/10-account-based-marketing-thought-leaders-follow/

https://www.itsma.com/research/

REFERENCES

https://www.itsma.com/enabling-thought-leadership-in-the-field-ibms-engagement-strategy/

https://www.ibm.com/thought-leadership/institute-business-value

https://www.ibm.com/services/insights/c-suite-study

https://www.cisco.com/c/en_in/about/thought-leadership/workforce-2020-what-to-expect.html